LAHORE
with love

LAHORE *with love*

Growing Up with Girlfriends, Pakistani-Style

FAWZIA AFZAL-KHAN

Syracuse University Press

Disclaimer: While this book is a memoir and, as such, based on real-life incidents, people, and places, it is nevertheless *my* recollection of these, hence more a matter of partial perception than "fact." Names of people and descriptions of some events have been changed/fictionalized to protect identities and privacy.

First Edition 2010

10   11   12   13   14   15   6   5   4   3   2   1

∞ The paper used in this publication meets the minimum requirements of the American National Standard for Information Sciences—Permanence of Paper for Printed Library Materials, ANSI Z39.48-1992.

For a listing of books published and distributed by Syracuse University Press, visit our Web site at SyracuseUniversityPress.syr.edu.

ISBN: 978-0-8156-0924-7

Library of Congress Cataloging-in-Publication Data

Afzal-Khan, Fawzia, 1958–

Lahore with love : growing up with girlfriends, Pakistani-style /

Fawzia Afzal-Khan. — 1st ed.

p. cm.

ISBN 978-0-8156-0924-7 (cloth : alk. paper)

1. Afzal-Khan, Fawzia, 1958–   2. Women—Pakistan—Lahore.   3. Female friendship—Pakistan—Lahore.   4. Lahore (Pakistan)—Social conditions.   I. Title.

HQ1745.5.Z9L332 2010

305.48'8914122009045—dc22   2009048717

Manufactured in the United States of America

To girlfriends, past and present

Fawzia Afzal-Khan is a professor of English and director of Women's and Gender Studies at Montclair State University in New Jersey; an author and editor of four books and innumerable essays of scholarly and political criticism on postcoloniality, performance, feminism, and Muslim women; and a published poet and playwright. To keep things interesting, she likes to sing, dance, and live out her wild-woman self in all its glorious, artivist madness. She lives with her husband and two children in Ossining, New York.

Contents

Foreword, CAROLE STONE | *ix*

Acknowledgments | *xi*

Introduction: *The Strangeness of Place* | *1*

1. Sam's Secret | *12*

2. Hajira | *33*

3. Saira | *59*

4. Blood and Girls | *76*

5. Mad/medea | *95*

Epilogue | *126*

Foreword

CAROLE STONE

Fawzia Afzal-Khan calls her book *Lahore with Love* a memoir. She is being modest. It is more complex than that. *Lahore with Love* is both a paean and a rebuke to Pakistan, the country of her birth. It is witness to violence against women, strictures of a patriarchal society, narrow-minded religion, and dictatorial government.

An additional complexity of Afzal-Khan's memoir is her use of a mix of forms. Both poetry and history provide forms of witness and, by interrupting narrative coherence, add emotional truth. Poetry interrupts narrative with emotional images; footnotes documenting the abuses of women and descriptions of the history of Pakistan's rulers reinforce her real-life stories, in which women sometimes overcome those abuses.

Afzal-Khan, who was born in Lahore, Pakistan, at the end of the 1950s, attended a convent school and later Kinnaird College for Women in Lahore where she and her girlfriends received a genteel English education. She and her friends—aspiring actresses, artists, and intellectuals—reflect the vestiges of colonialism, good and bad, as well as the early promise of Pakistan.

And what happened to those friends? Hajira gave up art in deference to her husband's success and later, at a dinner party, shot herself. Saira married a medical student when she was eighteen, had three children, lived through her husband's affairs, and had a nervous breakdown. Madina, aggressive and foul-mouthed, abused her husband and competed with Afzal-Khan in the theater and romantically. Samina's body is found on a bench in the garden of a hospital, a suspected "honor killing" by her brothers.

Blood as metaphor permeates Afzal-Khan's book. She learns about menstruation from Hajira who is bleeding and in pain. This discovery is linked to other images of her country, notably the civil war that resulted in East Pakistan's becoming Bangladesh. Afzal-Khan notes with rage and remorse the rape and killing of over 3 million people by the Pakistani army. She describes being caught in a late-night religious procession in which Shia men flagellate themselves to commemorate Hussain's martyrdom. Afterwards she screams at her mother who claims the Shia pollute wells with their blood after this ritual. A young woman, divorced from her abusive husband, who is assured she is safe in the office of Afzal-Khan's cousin, a human rights lawyer, is shot dead by her mother and a man who persuade a guard to let them enter.

Yet *Lahore with Love* is not unrelievedly grim. The writer's openness to experience, her love of men, women, food, theater, travel, adventure permeates her memoir. Her pain at what happened in many of her girlfriends' lives is balanced against the closeness they felt to each other, their love of literature and the theater, and their first stirrings of sexual desire. While Afzal-Khan escapes Pakistani patriarchal culture via American university degrees, marriage to a fellow Pakistani student, and U.S. citizenship, she never loses her involvement with Pakistan. Nor does she view the United States as a culture untrammeled by the strictures of patriarchal conventions and other political and ideological problems. She educates us about the history of the country she left behind and so ardently loves and hates. The intimacy and casualness of her voice with its appeals to "Dear Reader" seduce us and take us inside often horrific events, spinning tales even when we may not want to hear them. We are left in the present with the grown woman wondering what will happen next in her beloved Pakistan and in her life. For now, we have this deeply layered, wondrous story.

Acknowledgments

This book has been a long time in the making, for a variety of reasons. My teaching schedule, which involves teaching three courses each term and attending to the needs of my 75+ students a semester; my family obligations, which have included raising two children—quite grown now—and tending long-distance to my ailing beloved father who died a few years ago; my artistic commitments, singing and acting with the company I helped cofound, Compagnie Faim de Siecle, and following the theater work in Pakistan I wrote about in my book *A Critical Stage*. My own battle with breast cancer, which is five years in remission now, *allah shukr;* my activism-organizing colloquia and other events such as We Are Gaza at the Brecht Forum in NYC in March 2009, which brought together poets, musicians, playwrights, actors, filmmakers, and academics from around the world to "connect the dots" between Palestine, Iraq, Afghanistan, and Pakistan; my passionate involvement with the country of my birth—where I have sung, acted, worked with theater and other civil society activists over the decades, and in recent years, helped build a postgraduate program in postcolonial studies at Government College University and taught MA English students at Forman Christian College, teaching my students there to be themselves and acquire knowledge, even if it means crossing the seas and coming to the big bad West, as I encourage my students here to travel "East"! I have crisscrossed these borders between East and West all my life, in the hopes of shattering stereotypes

Acknowledgments

of the Other on both sides—to show that "bad" and "good" are relative terms, indeed spurious ones, as are "East" and "West," embedded in politics and hence subject to change. And change we must, especially at this critical juncture in our world's history.

This memoir is dedicated to the women I knew when they were girls, who knew they wanted change, a world different to the one they saw with all of its injustices around them. Names have been changed to protect their identities, and in the end, they live on in these pages as my memories, not as "real" people. What has been created in these pages is also now authorless, for along with Barthes, I agree that the text, once written, becomes the property of the readers, to do with as they wish; an excellent postmodern escape hatch from shouldering the responsibility for mistakes committed! In all seriousness, though, I can only hope that the text will inspire more stories, more moments of sharing, some of which will be at odds with the stories of this text, some that will extend them along different chains of signifiers. This is the best mode of life a scriptor can hope for at the moment of her imminent textual death. . . .

I must thank Mary Selden Evans, my patient editor at Syracuse Press, who believed in this project from the start and stayed with it. Gratitude to my friends, especially the girlfriends from the latter part of my life who have been such excellent readers and encouragers along the way, especially Edi Giunta (without whom this book would not exist), Carole Stone, and Norma Connolly. I wish to acknowledge the Writers' Residency at the Chateau de Lavigny, Switzerland, for allowing me the luxury to complete work on this manuscript. And of course, to my family who know what it is to M/other the Other.

Fawzia Afzal-Khan
Ossining, NY
May 9, 2009

LAHORE
with love

Introduction
The Strangeness of Place

So, I suppose you want to know how much is true, how much
untrue, and then we can do some sort of statistical analysis and
come up with a precise percentage and figure out where the
weight is. That, however, would go against my purpose, which is,
among a lot of other things, to ponder the blurry line between
novels and memoirs. Everyone knows that a lot of memoirs have
made-up scenes; it's obvious. And everyone knows that half the
time at least fictions contain literal autobiographical truths. So
how do we decide what's what, and does it even matter?

—LAUREN SLATER, from her memoir *Lying*

Having found a wonderful disclaimer as an epigraph to the art—and
artifice—of memoir in general, I can now proceed to etch a little map to
fill in the landscape within which the layering of emotional and literal
truths of my own memoir unfolds.

Factually speaking, I was born at the end of the 1950s, almost
exactly a decade after the inception of my country, Pakistan. In a way,
we have come of age together, my country of origin and I, though like
every younger sibling, I see my older sister's mistakes more clearly than
she can, even after she's committed them, and, even at times, while she is
in the process of going down the garden path. The year I am born, 1958,
brings Pakistan its first military dictatorship in the shape of a handsome

general, sandwiched in a snapshot between Ike and JFK, all three on top of the world, sporting smiles the Cheshire cat would have been proud of. Declaring martial law, General Ayub Khan bans all political parties, setting a precedent that leads to three more military overthrows of civilian–elected governments in as many decades. In 1971, while under the rule of yet another military dictator, Pakistan enters a war over East Pakistan with India and its own East Pakistani brethren, which ends with the ignominious surrender of 90,000 Pakistani troops and the creation of Bangladesh—the former East Pakistan. All this amid accusations of Pakistani army generals' debauchery and encouragement of rape and plunder by the troops under their command.[1]

While the secession of East Pakistan and the Pakistani army defeat leads to the end of General Yahya Khan's illicit rule, Z. A. Bhutto's democratic ascension to power does not stop the slide toward increasing sectarianism, nepotism, and widespread government corruption. Despite his socialist sloganeering, Bhutto amasses much personal wealth, disposes of his critics by arranging their kidnapping and murder, and presides over the process leading to increased power of religious extremists. I still remember with a sick feeling in the pit of my stomach the day

1. The number of civilians that died in the liberation war of Bangladesh is not accurately known. The casualty figures put forth by Pakistan (26,000 according to the Hamad-ur-Rahman Commission) vary greatly from those put forth by India and Bangladesh. The first postwar prime minister of Bangladesh, Sheikh Mujib-ur-Rahman, mentioned on several occasions between 1972 to 1975 that at least 3 million had died. The international media and reference books in English have also published figures which vary greatly—from 5,000 to 35,000 in Dhaka, and from 200,000 to 3 million for Bangladesh as a whole. Some believe that the figure of 3 million has its origin in comments made by Yahya Khan to the journalist Robert Payne on February 22, 1971, "Kill three million of them, and the rest will eat out of our hands." *The Guinness Book of Records* lists the Bengali atrocities as one of the top five genocides in the twentieth century (http://en.wikipedia.org/wiki/1971_Bangladesh_atrocities).

when Bhutto—so admired by us young folks with Che posters adorning our bedroom walls—declared, under pressure from religious parties, that Qadianis, a sect who till then had been considered—as they had considered themselves—Muslims, were heretics.[2]

2. In 1974, Zulfiqar Ali Bhutto, the prime minister, took the first major step to marginalize the Ahmadiyya community (also referred to as Qadianis) in Pakistan. He superintended the passage of second amendment to the 1973 constitution whereby Ahmadis were declared non-Muslims in the eyes of the law. He was later deposed and then hanged by General Zia-ul-Haq. Ten years after the passage of the Second Amendment, General Zia, the president and chief martial law administrator, promulgated Ordinance XX in 1984 whereby Ahmadis' freedom of faith was severely curtailed and it became a criminal offence for them to profess, practice, and propagate their religion. Three years' prison term was prescribed by the general for violation of the ordinance. The ordinance also conveyed that the state had adopted the persecution of Ahmadis as policy, and all branches of the government and the clerics were encouraged to follow up and implement the policy.

Although the general perished in a plane crash four years after the ordinance was passed, his policy regarding Ahmadis remained in place, and successive governments took no steps whatsoever to reverse the evil of the ordinance, which was incorporated in the Constitution in 1985 as a part of the Eighth Amendment. General Pervez Musharraf took over the country on October 12, 1999. He claimed to be a liberal and supported human rights in public utterances. However, beyond verbal support to an enlightened image of Pakistan under the new regime, the general took no initiative to undo the wrongs imposed upon Ahmadis. In September 2003 the general floated the idea of "enlightened moderation."

Recently, the UN General Assembly adopted on December 15, 2004, a Pakistan-sponsored resolution entitled *Promotion of Religious and Cultural Understanding, Harmony and Cooperation*. The resolution reaffirms the commitment of all states to fulfill their obligations to promote universal respect for, and observance and protection of, human rights and fundamental freedoms for all in accordance with the United Nations charter. However, Musharraf's government has been very selective in the application of this idea. Ahmadis have been deliberately and visibly kept outside the ambit of this policy. It is pathetic to note that only two weeks before the passage of this resolution in

In 1977, just as my girlfriends and I are preparing to celebrate our graduation from Kinnaird College for Women in Lahore, General Mohammad Zia-ul-Haq seizes power, arrests Bhutto, and declares martial law. As always when the army takes over, the Constitution is suspended. Colleges and universities are closed down indefinitely, our final exams get postponed, and, of course, there is no graduation. Not that year. I end up enrolling the following fall for a master's program in English literature at the prestigious Government College in my town. The year after, before completing my degree, I get a scholarship to the States for a Ph.D., and soon after I arrive on those distant shores that September 1979, I hear that Bhutto has been hanged, in a disputed conviction for conspiring to commit a political murder.

In 1980, as I immerse myself deeper into American graduate student life, the Soviets invade Afghanistan and the United States pledges assistance to Pakistan, which becomes the frontline state in a proxy war against the Soviet Union on its neighbor's soil. General Zia, in a bid to legitimize his power and strengthen the mujahideen fighters and later the Taliban

---

the UN General Assembly, an Ahmadi, Muhammad Iqbal, was sentenced to life imprisonment by a Faisalabad court on fabricated charges of blasphemy. The court believed the two false witnesses produced by a mullah against the Ahmadi accused who allegedly told them that their prophet was false. Only three months before this resolution, the police in Sindh charged fifteen Ahmadis under the Ahmadi-specific law as they were accused of writing *Bismillah* ("in the name of God") and *Assalamo Alaikum* (Islamic greetings), etc., on wedding invitation cards. The police arrested the bridegroom and his father. In February of the same year, the Election Commission was told by the government to reimpose the old policy of separate voters' lists based on religion and a declaration regarding end of prophethood in voters' application form. After the passage of this resolution at the UN, the government decided to stamp machine-readable passports with the holder's religion. Whither enlightened moderation and "protection of human rights and fundamental freedoms"? ("Persecution of Ahmadis in Pakistan during the Year 2004," Persecution .org, http://www.thepersecution.org/nr/2004/y2004.html).

against the Soviets, begins his Islamization drive in Pakistan, which includes funding hundreds of religious madrassas in the country and passing obscurantist, repressive laws aimed at curtailing the rights of women and religious minorities in Pakistan. This is the beginning of the end, the dawn of a new darkening chapter in the history of my motherland.

But as I record my memories of time spent growing up with my best girlfriends, sisters all, in spirit if not in flesh, it matters not if, Cassandra-like, I have sensed disaster coming their way, my way, my country's way. No one listens; no one sees. Not even one's own intuitive self. And so I write this memoir, in hopes that by giving voice to a past, the future of a present need not be so blind, so deaf, so very dark. As Eavan Boland, capturing the truth at a poetic slant, states, memory is a witticism in the face of terror.

In a patriarchal society, particularly a segregated one such as Pakistan's where male and female spheres of behavior and influence are clearly demarcated—in theory, though, as you will see, not always in practice—it is not surprising that same-sex relationships, especially for women, acquire deep, long-lasting emotional resonance. For me, growing up as the only eldest daughter of a middle-class urban Pakistani family, girlfriends became a lifeline supplying dreams of possibilities as well as warnings of dangers beyond the walls of my home.

My mother, despite being a college professor, was firmly anti-intellectual, and conventional in her expectations for me. "Don't read so much, you'll never land a husband," she would repeat to me. "Don't go swimming in the middle of the day, your complexion is dark enough already," she'd say with a withering glance. Being a darkie reduced further my chances at procuring a good *rishta,* or marriage proposal. "Cross your legs when you sit . . . smile pleasingly . . . don't talk so much," she'd admonish constantly, "and why don't you learn to sing something more pleasing than these classical ragas no one can appreciate." What she meant was, develop what talent you can to please the ears of those eligible bachelors, since what you have to offer the eye does not fit the standard of fair-skinned beauty. And woe to the girl who held opinions on matters philosophical and political . . . hardly the trappings of a suitable, moldable wife. And yet, here she was, the family chauffeur after Daddy's brain tumor operation when I was only six, earning her keep, contributing to the family income . . . a beautiful, opinionated woman, whose girlish figure and demurely flirtatious smiles drew many an "uncle,"—a "family friend"—to our home and to her company.

Dear Mother,

Recall that evening one hot Lahori summer? You were, I think, surprised by the events of the afternoon when I caught you red-handed, at least in my fertile imagination; you a little afraid, perhaps, of what the evening might bring while you were mingling with your dinner guests on the front lawn, all of them charmed by your red-sareed presence, fingering your food, dipping their fat little fingers in your savory sauces no doubt—I, perched shakily on the charpai's edge in the back verandah, told dad.

Recall now, in your hour of suffering as you tend to his defecations and urinations, how that man stood by you, swaying in the monsoon-laden wind that roared around the house that night, yes, but left him, and you, and the mango tree in our backyard still standing upright by day's end.

Oh, yes. We had "mixed" dinner parties often, men and women sitting together and chatting and laughing gaily, their sons and daughters often invited along so that we would have kids our own age to be with. Several of my closest girlfriends had no such gatherings in their homes, their households being far more strictly segregated than mine. And yet, what I had was not quite right. I mean, it wasn't like I could really have guy friends. As the teenage years hit, I could have girls over but not any boys, and when I rebelled and had some boys or young men visit. . . . Once I even had a young actor I had a crush on sit and talk to me in my bedroom; my mother slapped me after banging open my bedroom door unceremoniously, her face a clear sign for the poor young man to depart in a hurry as she screamed before he was even out of earshot, "How dare you take a boy into your room!"

No, my friend Hajira had the really cool family—she was allowed to hang out with her boy cousins as much as she wanted, they all went on long excursions together, and she was even allowed to enroll in the notorious mixed-sex Fine Arts College, where many of her friends were members of the opposite sex, including guitar-strumming, drum-banging cuties! Her parents were literary, westernized intellectuals, into music and art, whereas mine, even my philosophically-inclined father, tended to pooh-pooh all that "artsy-fartsy" stuff as pretentious at best and dangerously corruptive at worst.

Thus, unlike many American writers whose memoirs I have been reading lately, I did *not* wish to "belong" to what they describe as "the norm." I was the "norm," at least as far as outward appearances, in my society and culture. My father was not a drunken writer whose poet friends would pass out on their dinner table, leaving Anne Lamott, memoirist, wishing for the "normal" stable home life other kids in her American suburbia of the 1950s apparently had. Nor was my mother as visibly dysfunctional as Lauren Slater's, demanding a perfection it was not in the power of her daughter to give. Oh no. I was—despite my mother's angry attempts to curb what she perceived as my unconventional or rebellious behavior—assured of my own perfection, my special gifts for language, for music, for theatrical expression. The problem for me was that the others in my life at home were not similarly convinced—at least not to the degree I wished them to be! Dad adored me, it's true, and Mum, for all of her "do this, don't do that," did drive me around to French classes, to drama rehearsals, to music gatherings and catered to the needs of my music teachers. Still, I felt I was surrounded by philistines, and I needed someone, anyone, outside myself to tell me I was indeed special, different, deserving of greatness and the unusual, the abnormal, life.

I have traveled to seek the "different," "the exotic," that always elusive space of greatness, of liberation, which is also the space of untruth, of deception. I have traveled far and wide, so wide as to put millions of miles and several continents between my mother country and myself. What has sustained me, kept me grounded through all the flying about I've done in the past three decades, has been the memories. These are the memories of, and in some cases the continuing relationships with, the girlfriends of my earliest youth. A glittering diamond in the nose, Sophia Loren eyes, a bride in purple and gold, four girls in a car boot laughing up a storm on the Mall Road one winter night, hot parathas and egg flips, nuns in white habits, enduring marriages, infidelities, murder, depression, suicide. Girlfriends whose lives have both encouraged me to fly and warned me of the dangers of the enterprise that cost Icarus his life. It is through the writing of our shared herstories that I am finally learning the humility that could have saved that mythical flyer. The question is, will it save me?

Pakistan is a strange place. Not just in my memory but in reality; for once, the two coincide. A place where the spaces I know most intimately are more secular than their counterparts in that paean to secularism, the US of A. And yet, a place where fanatical extremism, intolerance, and xenophobia have deep roots, sometimes pushing their way aboveground in the least expected of spaces. And so it is that liberal, wine-drinking types will suddenly regress on the disco dance floor and confess innate West Pakistani superiority over the "short, dark, Bengalis." Bengalis still somehow occupy a villainous niche in our collective psyche even after it was us "superior" West Pakis who raped their women and committed all manner of other atrocities during the Civil War of 1971 that led to the breakup of the two wings of the country and the creation of Bangladesh. "Those damn Hindus," or those "damn Shias," or those "damn Qadianis, Christian blasphemers, girls who have no shame, those women who should be stoned for adultery, those girls who should have their noses cut off for having shamed the honor of their fathers and brothers, those girls who should be *kari,* killed for having run off with their lovers,[3] those sisters who must be encouraged to become doctors, teachers, good wives and mothers, even pilots and prime ministers, yes, and hijab-toting believers who will damn the rest of our souls who sleep around behind closed doors; and the fact is we love life, we love people of all different hues and religions and nationalities, let's welcome them into our homes and throw them lavish dinners, welcome, welcome, we are known for our hospitality, to even the gayest of flaming homosexuals (although those feminazi lesbians . . . umm . . . not so sure), the poor man will share his roti with me even though it is his only meal of the day. . . ." Of such excessive verbiage are dinner and dance conversations made at the most elite homes of La-(w)horites then and now.

---

3. In a section entitled "Harmful Customary Practices and Traditions," some of the anti-women practices are described as extant to this day in areas of Pakistan: "These include the selling off the girls in marriage, the exchange or barter of girls to settle disputes (*badl-i-suth*), the practice of Karo-Kari, siah kari and swara, marriage of girls to the Quran, the practice of giving girls to the Pirs to do or obtain a favor to get a cure done, the practice of Kammis held as bonded labour by landlords, and many other practices of similar nature. The price for a bride or walwar was reported to have risen up to Rs 30.000/- in Balochistan. The practice of swara in NWFP and tribal areas, or the handing over of young girls to rival parties to settle a dispute or conflict, continues and similar practices are also reported from Southern Punjab" (E. C. Pinto, Advocate High Court, "Women, Prostitution and Other Social Abuses," in *Status of Women in Pakistan 2000* [Karachi: Pakistan Federation of Business and Professional Women], 62).

Yesterday, today, and tomorrow, Pakistan is a strange place, where all of these sentiments and realities of differences in class, gender, and sexualities coexist in a bizarre palimpsest of history and synchronicity. I was born in this place of paradox, a place that is both home and abroad for me now in my life as a naturalized American citizen. This is a place where women are oppressed and where they resist without shame for the sun.[4] Where leaders are corrupt and the people generous and kind. Where women wear the hijab in ever-greater numbers and others dance almost naked at the most elite of clubs and homes. Where alcohol is banned in public and consumed at an alarming rate in private. Where young men commit suicide in response to increasing unemployment, while others drive Porsches and build homes in imitation of the White House.

My place is now also a place where I manipulate my Muslim womanhood to make my way up the U.S. academic ladder, reporting to increased acclaim the dire situation of Muslim women of Pakistan. My place is now a paradox of no-place, my home is now abroad, I have become exotic to myself, a stranger to my (s)kin. The paradox of this no-place I inhabit has been fundamentally shaped by the lives and friendships of the girls who were my closest confidantes, and by the women who have now taken their place, at home and abroad; it is this dis-ease of paradox that I now wish to share with you, in the spirit of a friendly exposure.

To make friends with disease. Battling breast cancer a few years ago, I picked up Susan Sontag's *Illness as Metaphor*. Fear of the unknown: that is what gives illnesses like cancer or AIDS power over people's imaginations, frightening them into believing in their invincibility.

4. *No Shame for the Sun* is an excellent sociological study of six Pakistani women representing different socioeconomic classes; Shahla Haeri, *No Shame for the Sun* (Syracuse: Syracuse University Press, 2001).

That is the gist of her argument as I understood it, or needed to, as I fought my way out of that disease. So, getting at the facts, you expose the beast for what it is: nothing but a dis-ease, which, seen through the pictures that words can paint, loses its power to frighten and overpower us. Expose the darkness of an ignorant negative to the cold hard light of a reasonable print: no shame for the sun, let's fly to the edge, embrace that paradox.

Does this picture seem too bright, dear reader? Sontag died recently battling a recurrence of the darkness she thought she had vanquished with the light of words. So perhaps you are right. I too find myself looking doubtfully at the print my memories have created, not sure at all about the grandiosity of redemption or hope or even of understanding. All I can do now is to implore you to enter this photograph, *mon semblable, ma soeur,* enlarge its dimensions, put it up on your wall. We are all in it together, I fear, but also, yes, in hope—secret sharers in the strangeness of place.

1

Sam's Secret

I think she is the loveliest thing I've ever seen: straight brown hair down to her lower back, like a chamois sheath I want to feel on my bare skin. She smells delicious too—her starched white uniform and spotless white canvas sneakers of a piece with the wafting aroma of chambeli flowers, a sweet-smelling fragrance that above all conveys a fresh powdery cleanliness on days when everything else seems to wilt into a stinky sweat except, of course, for Sam.

I first see her in the ninth class at the Convent of Jesus and Mary in Lahore, where, by May 1970, I have spent what feels like eternity in the company of nuns, a most natural place to be for all of us girls from respectable, middle-class Muslim homes. Are you puzzled, dear reader? Don't be. A convent school was indeed the place for middle- and upper-class parents to confine their daughters in a society that demanded that their girls be educated, yes, speak fluent English to be marriageable to the right kind of men—the educated ones, with good job prospects in the government ministries and civil services, or state banks like PICIC or IDBP, or who were doctors or engineers—but also be kept in segregated environments. Really, what better place to instill the virtues of virginal behavior than nunneries? Add to that the classes in cookery and housekeeping we all had to take; well, you get the picture . . . all in keeping with the colonial motifs of raising natives to conform to the best of civilized behavior and decorum as instilled in the various regions of the former British Empire.

Indeed, we latter-day Pakistanis, "free" from both Indian and British rule at the stroke of midnight, 1947, were, twenty years later, living proof of the successful indoctrination put into practice through the elite educational institutions following Lord Macaulay's infamous Minute on Indian Education a century ago. As we dutifully memorized and recited Shakespearean quotes like "Life is a tale told by an idiot / full of sound and fury / signifying nothing," we never thought the lines held any ironic connection to us. Macaulay had quite rightly predicted our own native mind-set all these decades later, as cultivated so assiduously by the nuns our parents entrusted gratefully with our care year after year: "I have never found one among them," he proclaimed gravely in 1838, "who could deny that a single shelf of a good European library was worth the whole native literature of India and Arabia." It was only natural that our Irish Catholic mentors made sure we were caned if we were ever heard conversing in any language other than English! No wonder I loved the English classics over any other literature in the world, and that to this day, I remain a stranger to my native-language literatures in Urdu and Punjabi.

Girls from the landed and business elites also attended these convent schools—Benazir Bhutto was a product of the Convent of Jesus and Mary Karachi, and later, of its boarding-school branch in the enviable hill-station town of Murree—then a resort for the westernized elite, now shunned by them in favor of more exotic locales "abroad," inaccessible to the "riff-raff" that has begun to frequent the likes of Murree and Nathiagali in the northern parts of Pakistan.

"God give us this day our daily bread, hallowed be thy name, thy kingdom come, and forgive us our trespasses as we forgive those who trespass against us . . ." Is that the order of the words we learnt by heart to recite every morning at the Great Assembly inside the big hall before our day at the school started? How many times does that mean we recited the Lord's Prayer? . . . I feel ashamed. I should be absolutely sure of the words, of their order, I, who spent eleven years of my life inside the convent walls, 7 to 2 every single day except for holidays. Heads bowed every morning, at first I would see red shoes with rounded toes and straps buckling them tight, encircling ankles wearing white socks attached to skinny brown legs for the world to see. We wore frocks—as they were called—white, with red belts clinching our waists, the bottoms all flared up as if we had can-cans on underneath. Did we? We couldn't have, surely. Such fashionable vanity would not have sat well with the nuns—who became our Mothers first, and then our Sisters. That change in nomenclature was dictated by the Catholic Church in all of its wisdom when we had transformed into grown-up young ladies, in the ninth class, the year Sam came to join us. By then, I can no longer see my ankles when I bow my head at the start of a school day. The uniform now mandates we be covered in appropriate Pakistani style, wearing the ubiquitous shalwar kameez, long shirts over baggy pants so our legs are covered, as Muslim custom demands. Instead of the red belt cinching in our waists, we now wear red sashes slung across our shoulders and pinned at our sides—a nod in the direction of covering our budding bosoms. I wonder how the nuns could get away with wearing habits that exposed their ankles . . . and Sister Cecille did have such pretty ones . . .

Sam has appeared as if out of nowhere, occupying the seat that has remained empty for almost half the year two rows over from where Hajira and I sit. We try to engage her attention through our usual show-offy antics while Baba Sahib drones on and on reciting Ghalib or Mir (do we care?), but she seems otherwise distracted—gazing off into the distance, dreamlike, unfocused. I still remember the profile; the aquiline nose, ever so slightly upturned, the arched brows, neatly plucked—while I still sport the bushy untweezed look of (I now like to think, though I hated it then!) a Pakistani Brooke Shields, since Mum hasn't permitted me to pluck out unwanted hair yet. What is she thinking about, wonder Hajira and I, our teenage curiosity piqued by the stranger in our midst.

Sam becomes our nickname for Samina once shy standoffishness has turned into familiar friendship, and inspired by the secretiveness of "S," Hajira, the budding painter-poet, decides she will be "Shelley," while I am given the name "Sindy," quickly shortened to "Sin," then lengthened again to "Madame Sin," an epithet that turns out to be prophetic. Only Amena, alias Hayley (Haji's older sister), calls me that anymore, reminding me of best friends long since gone, of an era when I fancied myself the swashbuckling center of a heartbreakingly sweet and sentimental universe.

Lulu sings "To Sir with Love" to Sidney Poitier, the perfect teacher who wins over the hearts and minds of scummy students with no real future but, at least for the girls, the promise of one made possible through the love of, and for, a "good man." It is a movie that our group of close friends—Haji aka Shelley, Amena aka Hayley, Saira, Honey, and I all get permission to see. It is the first time any of us has seen a black man—a Negro was the way we all referred to him then, not knowing any better—on the silver screen. Despite his blackness—anyone that dark was a no-no to our colonized aesthetic—we promptly fall in love with him. One afternoon, sitting atop our desks during a rare class period when our very old sir, our Urdu teacher, has not shown up, we are all thrilled when Sam begins to sing, shyly at first and then stronger as she hears our surprised oohs and aahs. She is very good at mimicking Lulu's lilting trills, her voice just as feminine as the rest of her, crooning "To Sir with Love . . . who has taken me beyond pencils and crayons . . ." while the rest of us gaze off into dreamscapes peopled by our own dashing "Sirs," beckoning us beyond the red walls of the convent, into the world outside.

But the outside is peopled only by pathetic creatures like the Hico Man, buckling over his ice-candy trolley, sweat pouring out of him like a burst geyser, the two-and-a-half hairs stranded on his egg-shaped dome wilting to a zigzaggy treacly mess under the fresh young bodies plastered all over him; hot, sweaty bodies demanding relief in the shape of lollies that refuse to hold their firm cold shape but instead melt away before the imploring tongues of hysterical girls get in even their first virgin licks.

Or the ambi-man, with his enticing kohl-rimmed eyes, a somewhat more promising prospect than the ice-lolly man, handing out khatta-khatta, raw mango halves the color of the Pakistani flag, coated in salt and cayenne pepper to burn the impure thoughts right off the tips of our salivating tongues . . . oh, how we learned to use those tongues to suck the sour sour juices right out of the milky white flesh cradled inside the hard green skins umumumyummmeee . . . but I was always sick after, and one humiliating year Mum found me out when she cleaned out my satchel after I'd been sick with a sore throat for a week—the skins were all shriveled and black looking, with only a telltale smell left to give away the secret.

Sam confesses conspiratorially to Haji, Honey, Saira, and me one fine day that she has a secret to share with us. This is a day like any other during the spring of the Civil War of 1971 that has left tens of thousands of East Pakistanis dead, butchered by their West Pakistani brothers while all we know is that we are at war with the evil Indians who want to tear "our" East Pakistan away from us. And here comes a secret involving men at war, oh my, or at least one man, her beloved (her what? our eyes big as watermelons), now in a refugee camp somewhere on the other side of the border, desperate to write her, to be reassured of the love of a good woman. Yes, we are women—almost—now, Sam, the oldest among us is nearly sixteen, Haji and I still the babies at fourteen . . . could we, would we, me, or Haji, be willing to receive letters from the beloved at our home address, so that the horrid, unsympathetic old-fashioned auntie Sam lived with wouldn't find out what was going on? Hajira and I have known of this witch-like aunt ever since we became friendly with Sam after her arrival at the convent, because in these couple of years we've never once been invited over to her place, nor has she been allowed to attend our birthday parties at our homes or go out to the occasional movie with us. Poor Sam, we always feel sorry for her, living without her mom and dad, who for some strange reason are living the good life in Germany while their daughter and her other siblings are forced to live stifling lives under the guardianship of their dragon lady phuphi . . .

So, of course, one of us has to say yes; and it is Haji, dear friend to the poor and the downtrodden, who agrees because she has the more liberal parents; parents who probably won't question the wherewhathow of swollen letters arriving thick as a plague of roaches; roaches that would appear unfailingly every monsoon season to carpet my mother's kitchen floor in the dead of night, a secret only I knew since I was the sole inhabitant of that house who awoke every night with the urge to get an ice-cold glass of water from the fridge, trying to slake a thirst of increasingly alarming proportions.

I am almost illiterate about the war, though thirsty beyond belief. And when the war starts, with "our" army from West Pakistan going in to the East Pakistani capital of Dacca to prevent "those rebels"— the majority of East Pakistani citizens—from taking control of their destinies—on March 7, 1971, I know something bad is going to follow, something that will not slake what now appears to be an unquenchable thirst for violence, a violence turned inwards, against ourselves. I realize, from conversations I overhear in hushed tones whenever Mum and dad's friends are over that there are some legitimate grievances held by our Bengali brethren. I recall one brisk early spring evening, not long after some news reports leak out that our army in Dacca has killed students and professors inside Dacca university dormitories—and razed the only Hindu hall, Jagannath Hall—to the ground killing what later turn out to be six or seven hundred residents; various aunties and uncles are gathered at my parents home talking in mournful tones about the "madness" of what now appears to be a full-scale civil war unfolding in front of us. Uncle Osman, one of Dad's oldest friends, and at the time vice chancellor of the Engineering University in Lahore, says in his quiet way, "It is true that since Partition we have treated our Bengali brothers as inferior, you know . . ." He coughs apologetically, not wanting to tread on any patriotic toes gathered in the company that evening. "You know, although they are the more populous wing of our country, we here in West Pakistan have consistently allocated more than three times their share of resources for ourselves."

"Pshaw," snorts Uncle Mobin from across the room, seated on Mum's golden tapestried sofa. He is the one who can always be counted upon to be the Voice of Punjab—er, I mean, Pakistan. "Those Bengalis are not, they never have been part of the martial races. That manly job has always fallen to us Punjabis . . . and if we are the defenders, the soldiers of this country, whyfore should we not get the best resource allocations?" Well, who could argue with such a rational mind? Mum, always uncomfortable at the thought that her dinner parties could go awry because of "serious" conversation, gets up and announces dinner. "And do let's talk about pleasanter topics, shall we?" she says, smiling. Her command is understood to mean it's time for me to leave adult company and for the grown-ups to turn their attention from the distant war—unfolding a thousand miles away after all, on the eastern end of Indian "enemy" territory from us—to pleasanter topics like who wore what at the last wedding everyone has attended. That would be Uncle Osman's oldest daughter Sana's, to the middle son of rich and handsome feudal lord, Chaudhury Shaukat Hussain.

Later that night, in a post-dinner autopsy, I hear my parents tut-tutting about Uncle Osman's "misplaced sympathies" for the Hindusympathizer Benagalis. "We never should have trusted them to stay true or committed to the idea of Pakistan, darling," I overhear Mother say to Daddy as they enjoy a cup of kava in the sitting room once the last guests have left. My father, the statistician, informs Mummy that, "the Awami League, the largest East Pakistani political party, led by Sheikh Mujib-ur-Rahman, has won a landslide victory, *janoo*, in the national elections." I can picture Mummy rolling her eyes disbelievingly, and then Dad, gently insistent: "The party won 160 of the 162 seats allotted to East Pakistan, and thus a majority of the 300 seats in the National Assembly. This gives the Awami League the constitutional right to form a government, whether we like it or not. It is Bhutto's lust for power which has led us into this war, dearest wife." What he could not have known then was that by December 1971, we, the mighty west wing of the country, would have lost the war. That East Pakistan would have seceded, and that it would be decades before we West Pakistanis would acknowledge the dastardly role of the Pakistani army in looting, killing, raping our brethren on the other side of India.

So then the letters, with Hajira the ever-faithful courier. Naturally, she grows closer to Sam during that period, our senior year in school . . . consequently I lose interest in Sam and the supreme silliness of true confessions . . . yuck! Who needs *that* when Kinnaird College for Women is within our reach? The excitement is heady; we are, at last, almost out of the nuns' clutches, we are Women now, though none of us know quite what that means, except, perhaps, more fun and freedom . . . and so, when the war ends, in December of our final year at the convent, we hardly even register the fact that we are no longer West Pakistanis but just Pakistanis. Oh yes, it is sad that we have "lost" our eastern wing—no one wants to acknowledge that our prime minister Zulfiqar Ali Bhutto's greed for power, leading him to refuse Mujib-ur-Rahman's legitimate demand for premiership based on his winning the largest number of votes in that year's elections, may have played some not so insignificant part in the disaster that led to the war and eventual secession of East Pakistan. Yes, all the real grown-ups seemed to have a hard time even saying the word "Bangladesh," and most do not want to talk about our army's atrocities committed against the thousands—possibly hundreds of thousands—of Bengali civilians, including the rape and torture of women and children. These were "just stories"—not to be believed, much less to be discussed in public. And most certainly not in front of us impressionable youngsters.

And so it was that we forgot about Sam's fiancé and all that drama from earlier that year, as we began to ready ourselves for the exciting world of Kinnaird College for Women.

And so it happens that I drag Haji to the auditions for our first annual play at Kinnaird, *The Ivory Door* by A. A. Milne . . . and wouldn't you know it, we both get in, me in a starring role of course—though never a female lead, oh no, I am chagrined to discover I shall be playing the silly old chancellor. I resign myself to the fact that being in an all-female college, things will not perhaps be so very different from the convent . . . I will forever get to play the male roles, and I curse my height and dark complexion for robbing me of the beautiful girlie parts. Still, being such a ham, I am happy to play a major character, and our rehearsals begin in earnest soon thereafter.

A gorgeous February afternoon, the kind that makes you want to curl up like a cat soaking up the sun's lemon rays, finds some of us doing our lazy cat impressions on KC's front lawn; out of the corners of my eyes, I see this petite Sam-looking young woman approach the group and ohmygod it IS Sam—only her luscious long locks are gone; she has a boycut (as we used to call it in those days) and and, ohgod, the love affair is over. He came back from the war . . . couldn't do it to his mom, you know, bring in an outside girl, his cousin's been patiently waiting all along . . . oh shit Sam, why'd you cut your hair? My heart is breaking while she, brittlely calm, smiles that beautiful smile not looking in the least like she's committed an act of vengeance. A strange kind of revenge, this, when you hurt yourself more than you hurt the object of your anger, and I realize only much later that such acts surely lead to one's own erasure. Little do I know that I am witnessing the beginning of a leitmotif of life with my girlfriends. But for now, I only want to scream at Saira don't start with your I told you so's, this is just lousy luck, but I too sense, perhaps, that she's right, they're all scum, bottom line, our world is not cut out for this boyfriend/girlfriend crap, boys will be boys and they'll marry Mama's choice, the girl with the locked up legs . . . I catch the hurt in Haji's Sophia Loren eyes and look away, come on, we've got a rehearsal to get to, upupup . . .

The play is a smashing success. But while I bask in the stardom I feel sure is my destiny, the real discovery of the play is Hajira. She has gone from spectator to participant in the space of a few short months, and wow, is she ever good . . . old man Beppo, my staff, my support (and we all thought I was the strong one!).

After the final performance on the third day, we have a visitor backstage. We realize immediately that she is Sam's older sister; she looks so much like her only, well, older, and not as pretty. Funny how that happens sometimes, a sibling will have the same features, but the combination just won't yield the same pleasing results. Anyhow, the plain sister is asking us, worriedly, if we've seen Sam. She has apparently not been home in the past three days—which was when we'd last seen her too, with her hair cut short—and none of us pauses to think how strange it is that Sam's sister hadn't shown up any earlier. I mean, think about it, why wait two days before investigating a disappearance? But since we haven't seen her since that fateful day-of-the-haircut, the sister leaves, and, flushed with youthful success, we all go back to the business of partying after the show.

The cast party ends late, Haji and I get home later than everyone else—we are the stars, after all—and I don't fall asleep until much much later, what with the performance-released adrenalin still pumping wildly. So, when Saira calls early the next morning, asking hysterically if I've seen the picture of the woman's body on the front page of the Urdu daily, I think for a brief moment that I am back on stage, only this time in a bad Urdu-language melodrama not the superior, more restrained English-language fare I've been involved in thus far. There is no doubt about it, however, no room for play; the dead body found on a hospital bench in the gardens of the Forman Christian Hospital is Sam's, looking for all the world as though she's just enjoying a catnap in winter sunshine on one of the park benches dotting the front lawns of Kinnaird.

Her house—or rather, her aunt's—is old and musty, situated in the lower-middle-class neighborhood of Garhi Shau, in an alley behind the convent. Not like the suburban homes Saira, Haji, and I live in, in the upper-middle-class enclaves of Gulberg, Cantonment, and Shah Jamal Colony, with their front lawns and garages, set back from the noisy thoroughfares of places like Garhi Shau where the toot-tooting of car and rickshaw and taxi and motorcycle and minibus and lorry-truck horns forms a constant background hum. Strangely enough, for an urban house, it is deathly quiet inside when we get there, and the verandah strip, with years-old choona peeling off the dampened, frieze-framed walls, seems to extend for miles before making a sharp turn left-wards to lead us into the inner sanctum, the zenana room now filled with women of all shapes and sizes, all much older than us mere babes in the wood. The air is thick with sobs and moans, some audible, others stifled at mouths stuffed with white duppata ends. Curious eyes look us over; we're all here, Hajira, Saira, Honey, myself.

Just as we're wondering where to go or what to do, a figure disengages from the amorphous mass of white. It is Sam's sister, we realize with some relief, getting up from the mourning women seated on the floor covered with white bedsheets, coming forward to meet us, so that we who are not yet schooled in the decorum of public grief and know not what to say or do, might dissemble our grief that has turned to embarrassment. Then, surprise of surprises, she introduces us to her mother, who turns out not to be this fashionable young creature groomed in the salons of the West as we had been led to imagine by our dearly departed friend, but a homely creature, quite old and fat. She looks just as puzzled as her older daughter when we inquire in our most grown-up manner after the mythical aunt, and even more so when we ask her how long since she got back from Germany.

In the midst of speechless confusion before anything can be satisfactorily explained, there is a commotion at the other end of the room. The wooden doors separating the world of women from the corrupt outside world are thrown open and two young men dressed in black shalwar kurtas with expressionless faces march in, bearing between them, on a charpai resting on their manly shoulders, the Dead Body. Everyone shrinks back except for the Mother, who, losing all self-control, throws herself, weeping and shrieking loudly, onto her daughter's corpse. I do remember mustering the courage to go up to the charpai on which she is laid out, wearing an outfit I recognized well: she had been wearing it that day when we last saw her. She looks so beautiful, eyes closed, that lovely nose upturned with the tiniest diamond stud in her left nostril glittering madly where the sun's rays filtering in from the roshandani catch it at just the right angle. I knew then that I would touch her, to feel that silky softness I had always imagined encasing me like a sheath; I was unprepared for the cold shock of freezer-hardened flesh that met my heat-pulsating fingers, leaving me with an awful case of freezer burn

I nursed for days afterward, licking my fingers over and over to lessen the numbing pain.

⌒⌒⌒

Weeks later, having discovered there has never been a dreaded "auntie," nor a picturesque "abroad" for cosmopolitan parents, five of us sit down to a séance in one of the Red Hostel's empty rooms. Looking for an answer that could do justice to our overheated minds and angry souls, we find it, Agatha Christie–style, in murder. While the rest of our classmates are poring over Camus's *L'Etranger* in Miss Alice's French lit class, Hajira, Saira, Honey, and I, joined by Hayley and the latest addition to our group, Naumana, commune with our friend on the other side, she who, as we'd found out so unpleasantly, had remained a stranger in our midst.

"Before we begin this—séance," says Naumana with some hesitation, turning her big, brown puppy-dog eyes to the rest of us, "I would like to understand a few things about Samina . . . Sam." Being the most impatient of the group, I am about to tell her to hold her questions till after, but Saira and Haji cut me off with their stares, and Saira gently intones, "Of course, ask what's on your mind, Nomi"—we are big on nicknames—"but remember, we are also much in the dark about so much concerning Sam . . ."

"Yes, I understand," nods Naumana, "but surely there is something very strange with the fact that she told you all her parents lived in Germany, that she had this terrible aunt—and why on earth didn't she tell you guys that she had a sister and brothers? I just don't get it . . . was she hiding something?" Silence hangs heavy like the stuffy, stale air in the hostel room we are in.

"We're not sure why . . ." begins Saira in her measured, rational way, but I jump in with my excited babbling, sure of myself as always. "Well, it's clear, isn't it?" I glare at the others, daring them to contradict me.

"She was ashamed of her lower middle-class roots. Her parents would never have allowed her to join in our fun and frolics, gadding about hither and thither all over town, riding in car dickeys and hanging out of car windows screeching at the top of our voices, watching who knows what manner of *fuhush* movies in the cinema halls."

Saira and Nomi both look uncomfortable at my broad-brush generalizations about class and illiberalism here. "Madame," admonishes Saira in her usual lecturing manner, "be careful what you say. My parents do not often allow me to join you and Haji and Hayley on these outings either . . . but that doesn't mean that they are backward"—she ignores my rolling eyes—"at the very least, it has not led me to lie to you all about the social limits within which I have to operate, nor made me cook up some crazy illiterate aunt to blame for my parents' seemingly old-fashioned beliefs."

She stops, and looks straight at me, daring me to challenge her. Right on cue, I lash out angrily, "What else do you call this nonsense about you can't do this and you can't go here and all the time that brother of yours can come and go as he pleases?"

"Oh Madame, when will you ever learn, this is our way, and it's a good way . . . our parents are only protecting us . . . see what happened to Samina for defying her family and culture's traditions and morals."

"Ohmygod, are you saying she did this to herself? That her death is her fault?" Now I am off the charpai on which we were all sitting huddled up, I am up and shouting, I can positively feel the foam gathering in my mouth.

Naumana's eyes seem to have dilated another inch; they are bigger than the *pirchis* on which our chai mugs rest. I think she is regretting what she's started. But I am in no mood to back off now. "Calm down, Sin . . ." and Haji's quiet voice has now entered the fray. She reaches out with her freshly waxed brown arm to touch me, to pull me back to the edge of the charpai. "Come on, *yaar*, no need to get so heated up," she smiles gently.

Honey, who hasn't said anything yet, speaks up, slowly drawing out her words in her usual Socratic fashion, living up to the intellectual label we have assigned her. "We don't really have many facts to go on to help us out of the muddle that was Sam's life. Do we?" She looks at us. "No. I didn't think so. The only fact we share is that none of us bothered to ever go over to Sam's house—and no"—before any of us could protest—"we did not have to wait for an official invitation. She lived close enough to school, for God's sake . . . any one of us could have just popped in after school. Sam may have appreciated the gesture as one of solidarity for her kind . . . I mean class . . ."

I snort at this. "You forget, dear Honey, that Sam never wanted us to come over her house. She always said her *phuphi* did not like any of her friends coming over. Are you suggesting we should have forced our way in?"

Nomi jumps in at this point. "So really, what you all are saying is that all the stories you have—or don't—about her family situation, came to you from Samina, without any corroboration of the facts. And none of you ever knew what was the truth there. For all you knew, Sam was a liar—as it would now appear—and probably a psycho!"

Realizing she may have gone too far in maligning our dead friend, Naumana looks stricken, and says she's sorry, she didn't mean to be so judgmental. Feeling the need to get back on track with our séance, I try to synthesize our limited knowledge at this point—I am suddenly tired of this back-and-forth on Sam and her motivations for telling us fabricated stories about her past and present. I realize with a pang there would be no future to her life story. "Listen, friends," I begin, trying to sound amicable. "The truth is that we have no truth here, except what we can glean from the circumstances of her life and manner of grisly death." Gosh. Looking back, I guess I was a poststructuralist avant la lettre! I can feel five pairs of eyes looking at me expectantly. "Except what we saw. And what we saw were brothers . . . angry brothers, who would not meet the gaze of any of the women in that room. Brothers she never told us about. Maybe they were the reason she could never go out with us . . . that she had to be so sneaky when it came to her love affair."

In the room whose windows we've darkened with borrowed sheets and bedcovers from some of our friends who board in the hostel, we share a collective shiver when Sam's spirit, captured under the bottle cap, goes zigzagging wildly all over the homespun ouija board, tripping over M-U-R-D-E-R, then spelling out "B-R-O-T-H-E-R N-A-M-E-D Z-A-H-I-D" with such speed our fingers can barely keep up with the top. The air suddenly turns deathly cold.

I remember Saira's nasal laugh puncturing our state of shock. She laughs loudly, always the practical spoiler of the bunch; Honey's face acquires that famous smirk, intellectualizing everything as usual; Hajira is the most visibly moved, Hayley her older sister following suit; while Nomi merely looks bewildered. I maintain a healthy skepticism in the absence of proof, wondering what the term "honor killing" really means, since prior to our sitting down to the ouija board, we all have bandied about that possibility without understanding what we are vocalizing. The answer on the board merely confirms our suspicions, rooted, I start to sense, in customs more ancient than our modern education or bourgeois backgrounds can easily comprehend.

I did, unbeknownst to the others, make a few calls to the home of the deceased after the ouija-board incident. Feigning a different voice, I asked to speak with Zahid to see if, indeed, Sam had a brother by that name; the female voice on the other side, which I couldn't quite place, hesitated a moment before asking, "And why do you wish to speak to him?" That was enough for me; I banged down the phone. A day or so later, I started receiving calls from a Christian friend of Sam's from the old convent days whom I hadn't seen or been in touch with after she'd dropped out of school in tenth class. She kept asking if I'd meet her downtown at this (very shady) Chinese restaurant because she had some stuff regarding Sam's death that she wanted to share with me; she wouldn't do it over the phone, nor would she give me her telephone number. Scared, I kept putting off the date; then, as suddenly as they'd begun, the calls stopped.

∞

It has taken me the rest of my life, literally, to figure out what could have happened. The year is 1999 AD, or 600 AH according to the Muslim calendar. Pakistan has recently celebrated its fiftieth anniversary, with the pomp and circumstance usual at such times in the history of nation-states. But for those who are at best its second-class citizens, women whose status has devolved rather than evolved with the passing of time, this is a year of deep reflection on how things could have gone so wrong. Through my postdoctoral involvement since the late 1980s with women's rights NGOs (which have become an important part of the Pakistani nongovernmental and civil society landscape) and with theater activists whose plays have increasingly been about human rights violations against women and religious minorities, I am newly aware of how dire things have become, perhaps always were, for at least half the population, in the country of my birth.

Maybe I misspeak. After all, the constitution of 1965 not only guaranteed separation of mosque and state, it also gave women the right of divorce, the right to choose their marriage partners, as well as inheritance and voting rights not previously encoded in the law. And while this was a secular constitution, the fact is that the rights accorded women as well as to religious minorities (4 percent of Pakistanis are Christian, and maybe 1 percent Hindus)—to worship freely and to run for the highest offices in the country save those of prime minister and president—were in keeping with the spirit of justice on which the Quran rests.

∞

Perhaps it was never really a matter of law, but of the privilege of class and clan. In the ignorance borne of class privilege, and despite the secret of Sam, I remember reading the novel *The Pakistani Bride* with a sense of dismay, and thinking, how could this woman be writing such rubbish, selling her culture out to the highest bidder of "exotica" in a society (the United States) already prejudiced against us? The novel, an account of a woman condemned to death by her own brothers for the crime of falling in love, is written by a Pakistani-American writer who later became a good friend. I remember thinking she had a really vivid imagination when she swore to me that women in our part of the world actually, really, truly swear-upon-god-and-hope-to-die had their noses cut off as punishment for bringing dishonor and shame upon their families by hinting desire for a man not picked out by their clan, or for refusing marriages to men old enough to be their grandfathers.

And so, it is the winter of 1999, a season of discontent that continues even after the oppressive ten-year reign of the late general Zia-ul-Haq ended in a mysterious airplane explosion in August 1988, killing the general and many of his top aides as well as the ambassador and top military personnel from the USA who were traveling with him in the shared intimacy of power. A man into whose ear God spoke directly, our beloved generalissimo had, with the stroke of a pen and the acquiescence of the mullah types he stuffed the houses of parliament with to give him the legitimacy he so desperately desired, gotten rid of all the laws meant to protect the rights of women and minorities.

Ramming the Eighth Amendment through Parliament and the courts, Zia effectively replaced the secular constitution of 1965 with one supposedly based on Shari'a—Islamic doctrine. This ensured that Christians and Quadianis could be defamed as blasphemers by neighbors

coveting their properties and condemned to death by stoning or hanging; that women bringing rape charges against their rapists would be
thrown into jail instead, accused of adultery or fornication unless they
could produce four adult male witnesses to the act of rape. Their testimony—and worth—reduced to half that of a man's—grown women
now needed their male guardians' permission to marry. And all in the
name of a putative "return to Islam," making the feudal chieftains and
landlords, who had always enjoyed coercion and rape of poor farmers
and tenants and their womenfolk as a birthright, happy and secure in
their power now so conveniently sanctioned by God.

And so. It is February 1999. My cousin-aunt, Asma Jahangir née Jilani,
has become a world-famous human rights activist and lawyer defending
the rights of women and minorities in a climate increasingly hostile to
both. She is sitting in her third-floor office in the building on Main Bou-
levard that houses AGHS, an acronym for the initials of the four women
who founded the Legal Aid cell set up in the 1980s to provide counsel,
shelter, and defense to women trying to escape their abusive family situations, which have been made ever more unbearable since the passage of
the (so-called) Shari'a laws. A young woman sits across from her desk,
light-complexioned I imagine as Pathans are wont to be, red-hennaed
hair pulled back from her face in a thick braid, her hazel-colored eyes by
turns calm and fearful as she looks over her shoulder every so often.

"Relax," I can hear Asma saying kindly in a voice surprisingly strong
coming from a slightly built woman. She chews on a wad of paan leaves
and beetlenut, the red paste of the katha staining her mouth and lips.
"You are safe here, Samia, and you know that the safe house you've been
staying at since you got here is in an undisclosed location; only a few
trusted staff know where it is. . . ." Her voice trails off as Samia begins to
breathe more slowly, her shoulders visibly relaxing.

"You are right, madam," her tone halting at first, then gathering more force, "of course you are right, because I feel so much freer since I escaped from my parents' house in Peshawar, and the nightmares are receding a little bit more each day." She bites her lower lip as her eyes glisten with unshed tears she is desperate to hold back.

I can just see Asma leaning across her wooden desk, awash with papers and file folders, to touch the young girl's fingers as they tap a nervous rhythm on the outer edge of the desk. "They have no legal power over you, Samia, no right to insist you go back to an abusive ex-husband instead of marrying another man of your choice. You are a twenty-four-year-old woman, legally divorced, and you have every right to marry again, without the necessity of parental consent. Do you understand that? We still have some rights left in this god-forsaken country of ours, this business of requiring the *wali's* consent is something we can still challenge in the secular courts." Realizing she may have gone too far with the god-forsaken part, Asma stops and says gently, "And please, stop calling me 'madam'; I'm not a schoolteacher, you know." She is pleased, I think, to see Samia responding with a smile that I am certain makes her look as though she is fifteen.

"I am her mother, please, I know she is upstairs with the lady lawyer," pleads the woman in the big chador, its *palloo* covering her head. "Please, you've got to let me pass, I have to see my daughter, the apple of my eye," now wiping her eyes with the edge of her chador. Sensing the guard's hesitation, she presses on: "I prayed for her all through Hajj, you can see, I even fell victim to the crush of pilgrims rushing to Mount Ararat," pointing to her right leg encased in a cast. "I have made my peace with her decision, I swear to Allah, and I have come to tell her this, to beg her to come back home to us, and she can marry whomever she chooses."

The guard, rifle in hand, must be embarrassed at this confessional outburst, and gruffly tells her she can go up, "but not the man who is with you, we are not allowed to let strange men go up."

"But he is my brother-in-law, Samia's favorite uncle, and as you can see, I need him to help me up the stairs, I cannot walk by myself."

Poor guardsman. I pity him at that moment, knowing that as a non-*mehram*, a non-relative of this woman, he cannot offer to escort her himself, and besides, his job requires he stand guard at the door. In that split second of wavering will, the uncle, dressed in traditional garb with a black chador concealing his torso, pushes his sister-in-law past the guard, holding her arm in one hand. Did the guard sense something? Did he think he should have stopped the pair from moving up the stairs at a speed much too fast for a woman with a broken leg? Did anything really register with him or was he consumed by twelve o'clock hunger pangs or by the need to empty his bowels? Or maybe the uncle had flashed him a secret sign, one Pathan man to another.

Before the startled daughter can run into her mother's arms opened wide in a gesture of embrace and forgiveness, before Asma can say Stop! It's a trap! one, then two, then three shots ring out. The first gets Samia in her head; the second, in her heart; and the third, clean through her crotch.

Uncle and Mommy abscond very fast, having grabbed a legal aide worker from the office as hostage. They get out of Lahore unharmed, dumping the shaken worker at Faletti's hotel on Mall Road, and make it back to the safety of their fiefdom in Peshawar, where the murdered girl's father, a prominent leader in the community, declares to all the world in the morning papers, "God's will is done." The mother, a lady doctor, presumably goes back to tending her female patients.

Maybe the ouija board that sad cold day in 1977 really did reveal Sam's secret to us in what was then the Newland of our youth; our Age of Innocence, now gone forever.

2

Hajira

*A*nd so the story begins . . .

I have just been double-promoted into class 8. Having been away—abroad—even though it was just Africa, Land of the Darkies—still, having had the privilege of studying with white colonial leftovers there, superior in every way to the many local dark-skinned nuns at my Lahore convent—I am now considered to have become "advanced" in some important way; enough, that is, to qualify me for a double-promotion. Sweet smell of success! After those early years of humiliation—class 2, class 3, class 4, class 5—being just your average Jill Schmo, almost-recipient of the infamous Pink Card (for "talking too much"), banished to the corner with the dunce cap once too often—oh, this is tooo delicious for words! I ready myself with extra care that morning in September 1969 . . . sparkling white PT shoes and socks, starched white *shalwar kameez* with the red sash pinned neatly to my flat chest, my thick blue-black hair tamed of its usual unruliness by Mom's strong hands twisting it into tight braids framing both sides of my face . . . yes, I look the very picture of seriousness, going off to redeem myself in front of all those Big Girls.

I hadn't counted on Hajira, though. I mean, this was supposed to be *my* moment; I was going to be the target of the older girls' envy. Goddammit, who was this shrimp, this pipsqueak, and Jesus Christ, what big . . . protrusions she has on her chest, a midget with melons oh gawd! Of course, on the surface, I was calm as a lake: *hello, how do you do,*

I'll only turn eleven on September 12, what did you say? Oh, right, your birthday isn't till October and you'll turn eleven too . . . well, yes, I guess that makes you even younger than me . . . isn't it funny, two new girls— well, I'm not exactly new to the school, you know, just to this class—but yes, fancy that, both of us, the youngest members of the class, oh sure, I'll be your friend . . .

Bummed out as I was at having the title of Youngest Student stolen from me by this upstart freshly arrived from the back of beyond (well, that's how we thought of Quetta, provincial capital of remote Baluchistan), we did, despite my initial huffiness, become friends. And what a friendship it turned out to be! How do I begin to piece together an era, a bygone age that disappeared almost three decades ago, yet seems as though it was here just yesterday . . . so close I can touch it, feel it, smell it . . . her . . . her body all womanly curves outstripping us all and her hair shiny and silky and full of the bounce of a shag . . . she plays with licking those thick lips as she flashes her Sophia Loren eyes, her nose's crookedness giving her a gnomish look that her petite size accentuates . . . she seems content though. I have the straighter nose and the height, but no boobs to speak of, so I guess we are evenly matched after all . . .

I am not allowed to sleep over at girlfriends' homes, even if, like Hajira, they don't have older brothers to seduce innocent teenage girls like me. Hajira's parents are considerably "cooler" than mine and a whole lot more liberal (perhaps because her mother is from the old aristocracy of Lahore, descendants of the Muslim freedom-fighting literary editor of a famous political newspaper of the 1940s and '50s, friend to the Founder of Pakistan, Mohammed Ali Jinnah), and they allow her to sleep over at my place off and on.

It's on one of these desperately desired and looked-forward-to occasions when intimacy grows by leaps and bounds that Hajira educates me about the Guest. She'd been acting a bit weird all evening, her usually energetic spirit oddly lackluster, refusing to stroll outdoors and instead just lying on my bed and writhing uncomfortably from one position to another. I ask her what's wrong, but she just readjusts the pillows and says *oh nothing, just a stomach ache* . . . so I carry on with my animated description of Samir who she hasn't met yet but already has a firm opinion about . . . *he's a chaaj, a creep, eeouw, how could you like someone like that, Madame Sin* . . . but today, she isn't responding much save for a sardonic smile and an occasional roll of the eyes. Finally, she sits up, moaning and groaning, telling me it's time for her to go change her Moddess pad because the Monthly Guest had arrived that morning. *What? I say . . . what the hell is a modest pad? What monthly guest?* Well. She looks at me with those beautiful slanty eyes, purses her lips and knits together her recently tweezed eyebrows (something I haven't mustered up the nerve to attempt yet)—answers, "It's time you learnt a few facts of life, Madame. You've been sheltered for far too long . . . I'm surprised your parents, especially your mom, hasn't told you anything yet . . . I mean, what if the same thing that happened to poor Mahnaz the other day in school were to happen to you?"

Now I'm shocked. Why would the same thing happen to me? I mean, I thought she had some sort of terrible disease—people don't just start bleeding uncontrollably for no apparent reason, do they? I shuddered, remembering the reddish-brown stain on the back of Mahnaz's white kameez, which looked innocuous enough when someone first noticed it but then spread like the plague itself to claim her entire backside. She held her red book bag behind her back, trying to block our stares as she was led out of the classroom fifth period by Sister Teresa, her head hanging low, as though she was terribly ashamed. I looked around and saw embarrassed looks on the other girls' faces, which I thought mighty strange at the time—I mean, shouldn't everyone be looking concerned and worried instead? But then lessons resumed, and somehow, Mahnaz and her plight vanished from my thoughts, only to be rudely dragged out of some deep recess of my mind by Hajira's comments now.

Moddess pads, I come to know, much against my will, are the sanitary napkins of choice. The name irks me to this day, with its not-too-subtle "subliminal" message exhorting women to be models of modesty. Hell, I was never going to be *that*. I think my desire to rebel against such injunctions of propriety may properly be traced to that fateful encounter with female blood, oozing out uncontrollably, big, dark clots plopping out of Hajira as she sits on my pink girlie potty making of me an unwilling witness; she insists I watch so that I can get over what she senses, correctly, is my aversion to "reality." I watch, all right, and witness her pain all night long; how she writhes, my poor Haji, how she moans and clutches her stomach curling up tighttighttight while I lie next to her, unable to do a thing except feel guilty that I haven't experienced the fall from grace yet, the soiling of my body that would lead to the pain of childbirth yet to come. I am consumed by feelings of fear and revulsion wondering if I'm going to wake up engulfed in sheets of blood.

The next morning dawns bright and sunny, albeit with a frosty nip in the air of a quality I've only experienced in Lahore on chilly December mornings that herald the onset of the cold foggy season; a clear sunny day despite the nip becomes a joy to cherish. Despite Haji's gloomy reluctance—her pain even severer than yesterday—I make her get up and take a walk with me on the dew-covered lawn of my parents' house in the still-suburban cantonment section of town. Oh those winter mornings! The temperature could not be less than 30 degrees centigrade, but getting out of a warm razai, soft quilt covers filled with layers of the purest cotton wool that wrapped us in their cocoon-like embrace so that emerging from under them into an icy bedroom required enormous willpower—well, that took some work. My bedroom felt like the inside of a Frigidaire most mornings—unless I had somehow sneakily managed to let the electric one-rod heater run all night, without Mummy popping in to double-check at some point during the night that it was off. "How many times must I tell you to shut off that heater!" she'd yell at me whenever she'd catch the heater on. "It is expensive to run it all night long and it's dangerous—with power surges in the circuits the rod could catch fire." How it might do so I could not understand, but who wanted to argue, especially with Mummy in one of her righteously indignant moods. That morning was an exception, though. Mummy must have relented and not checked in to see the obvious—must be the famed eastern hospitality, making sure your guests or your kids' guests are always comfortable . . . anyhow, its 8 a.m. I need to pee, and once I am up, I want Haji to get up too.

She resists, complaining of pain, but I am firm. "This will do you good, Haji; exercise gets the blood flow going and should relieve your cramps." I am amused to hear myself sounding like an expert. Like I would know. Haji turns to fix her sardonic glare on me—but I am ready; I defy her to defy me. She knows that look of determination on my face. She groans, but complies. "Okay, okay, we'll try your way . . . but only if I can bring my razai with me . . ."

Round and round we go in my parents' L-shaped front lawn, arm in arm, painting a funny picture I'm sure—Haji wrapped from head to toe in my rose pink razai with the powder-blue border and golden trim; and me, towering over her five-foot frame by a whole five inches, wearing my purple flannel pajamas and a matching Wee Willie Winkie nightcap on my head . . . what a pair, engrossed, as we always were, in never-ending conversations about everything and anything, pain or no pain. That morning's conversation, though, I remember as vividly as though it was yesterday. It was about the power of mind over matter. To every moan of Hajira, "I really can't, I really can't Ireallycan't . . ." I respond, "Yes you can, yes you can, yesyoucan . . ." After twenty minutes of this exchange, Haji is my Hajira again, standing upright and smiling.

With the bottoms of our canvas sneakers wet with dew from the grass, we go in to the glass-enclosed verandah at the rear of the house that serves as a breakfast room, since it is here that the sunshine comes in first thing in the morning. We sit down at Mummy's red-and-white gingham-covered table to a hearty Punjabi-English breakfast of egg flips and fried parathas, the latter crisp and hot fresh off the griddle just the way we like them. The egg flip, taught to us in cookery class by Miss Colin as a remedy for all manner of ills, is disgusting conceptually—I mean, raw eggs in hot milk? But I insist in my most maternal mode that Haji gulp it down. She obliges while making the requisite grimaces, but then smiles divinely after she's done and claims she feels as strong as a Punjabi ox. I smile too, happy in the knowledge that I have contributed in some small way to her acquisition of strength. Damn if I'll let blood between my legs ever rob me of mine!

Hajira teaches me many things. I would never have heard of Leonard Cohen, or Janice Ian, Crosby, Stills, Nash and Young, or even Simon and Garfunkel if it hadn't been for her and her older sister, Hayley. James Taylor's "You've Got a Friend," became our theme song; we swore we'd be there to the end for each other, sisters forever . . .

Hajira's mom and dad are the coolest parents I know. They listen to classical music (western, of course), and talk about Eliot and Lawrence and Picasso. I don't think my parents have ever heard these names. Or if they have, they don't discuss art and literature and music in our house—even though my mum is a professor of English at a well-known college for women. I've seen Harold Robbins on her bedside table—and when it's annual exam time, she reads Cliff's Notes to the novels and plays she's taught her students all year long so that, she tells me, she can design questions they will be able to answer without actually having read the works!

Haji's aunts and uncles and cousins are just as hip as her parents. Izzi—as her cousin Zahoor is commonly known—is her khala's only child, a doted-on son. He is much older than us, in his late twenties while we are barely into our teens, and whenever he visits from Karachi life becomes ever so exciting for us. I have to think up all sorts of excuses for how to get out of the house, and what is so great is that Hajira's parents and aunt often come to my rescue by conveniently omitting to mention to my parents that there will be boy cousins at family picnics and other outings that I am invited to go to with them.

A leisurely Sunday drive to the family's mango farm on the outskirts of Lahore, past Kot Lakpat, past the rolling green fields with young wheat stalks and rows of corn freshly planted, old Shaukat the driver told to get off at the bus stop and go have a lassi while Izzi takes the wheel despite the old man's protests, "Nahin, sahib, ammi abba naraaz hon gain . . ." We tell him to relax, the grown-ups will not miss us at the picnic, we'll be in an adjacent spot, they would never find out we made you get off . . . and then, we're off! Izzi drives like a maniac, and Haji and Hayley and I take turns sitting on the open window sill in the front of the car, screaming, "Viva Che!" putting our fingers up in the "V" sign at passing motorcycles, cars, buses, rickety rickshaws, horse-drawn tongas and the like, so in love with our hipness and imagined freedom. Mohsin and Fareeda, Auntie Jallo's kids and also related to Haji, are in the backseat, smoking Camel Lights and beating imaginary drums to the sounds of Jethro Tull blasting from the car's cassette player.

We do, eventually, catch up with the grown-ups, and tell them how the driver had developed a sudden but dreadfully painful stomachache, and so, to help the old man out and save our noses from having to smell his noxious farts, Izzi graciously offered to relieve him from his duties. Our story is met with some skepticism but the noxious-fart part makes every one giggle, and so all is well. And then we all sit down to a most delectable lunch of finger sandwiches filled with cucumber-and-tomato paste, egg salad and hunter beef; there is lovely fresh-squeezed anar juice (pomegranates being in season), and cheese straws and minced chicken patties, boiled peas and potatoes for Khala (who has delicate digestion, I am told, in a surreptitious whisper by Hajira). I am in seventh heaven; this is all so wonderful, so very different, and the food and delicate digestive tracts so much classier, than the *paratha-anda, biryani,* and *shami kebab,* local spicy, greasy, fare my family of the tough Punjabi stomachs indulges in when picnicking once a year at, of all places, Lawrence Gardens (where everybody, but *everybody* goes).

Lunch over, we "youngsters" as the grown-ups call us fondly, take off for a walk along the reed-fringed banks of the Ravi, whose muddy waters flow rather sluggishly beside us but appear nevertheless as a romantic symbol to our young, ardent eyes. While Izzi, Fareeda, Hayley, and I form a giggly foursome bent on walking a brisk mile, Hajira and Mohsin seemed to have paired off, falling more and more behind as the rest of us speed off, competing to see who would reach the far end of the riverbank first. When the four of us regroup, Hajira and Mohsin are nowhere to be seen, and so naturally, we begin to gossip about the possibility that they have fallen in love. "How absolutely *chooch* that would be, Madame," Amena aka Hayley exclaims excitedly in my ear. Izzi smiles enigmatically, saying something about poetic soul mates, while Fareeda, Mohsin's sister, blushes and recites some line about the marriage of true minds that eludes me but certainly catches Izzi's attention, and then the two of them are talking about Shakespeare and Tennyson and Shelley and Byron and I feel more lost than ever, cursing my mom, the fake English professor if ever there was one, wasting her life teaching stupid Urdu-medium lower-class girls who couldn't spell literature if their lives depended on it, while here were the cultured gems of our society, and all Mum and Dad did was to criticize their decadence and out-of-touchness with the rest of Pakistani society. But I push such angry thoughts about my parents' philistinism aside to join in our teenage communal reverie, fantasizing about love's possibilities amidst green fields dotted about with the mud huts of illiterate peasant Punjabi farmers, hut walls covered in a sprawling alphabet of cow-dung cakes used as fuel so out of sync with our bucolic Wordsworthian dreams . . .

∞

I'm dreaming of Hajira, lying on the soft green grass in her parents' lawn in the little white house they lived in when Uncle Hashmi was assistant superintendent of Ganga Ram Hospital . . . Emma is licking her face and Hajira is letting her drool spill all over her. Emma, what a name for a Pakistani mutt; obviously, Haji has read one too many Jane Austen novels. The sun is warm and toasty, just the way we like it on a winter afternoon, before the evening cold reminds us of the season we're in. Amena, dear old Hayley, older sister not just to Haji but to me too, comes out to call us in for tea . . . a drink with jam and bread I sing, and we're off, synchronizing and harmonizing Julie Andrews popular hits, what a choral team we are . . . Uncle and Auntie clap delightedly as we collapse giggling onto the comfy living room couch, whose sage green chintz pattern, now that I think of it, really does resemble those famous curtains from the *Sound of Music*. We eye the delicious chicken patties hungrily as we reach first for the pink-and-white-frosted pastries we picked out earlier that afternoon when the cake-and-pastry vendor had come clanging his wares in a steel case slung across his broad Pathani chest, interrupting our girlish frolics on the lawn with his unmistakably masculine presence . . .

∞

Mohsin had long ago (well, a year, to be precise) been relegated to the realm labeled "Silliness of Youth" by mature, nineteen-year-old Haji when she met Sufi—whose real name was Farooq—in her second year at art school. It struck the rest of us as hilarious that "Haji" should have met "Sufi"—"Haji" being a nickname we had coined to tease poor Hajira for having had the ill luck of being given such an old-fashioned, Islamic name, and the appellation, denoting one who has performed the sacred pilgrimage to Mecca, stuck. *(Fancy the chances of a haji meeting up with a mystic, we chuckled, pleased at Fate's mnemonic games.)* While the rest of our girlish gang—Saira, Nomi, Honey, and myself—had remained at the safely elite all-women's liberal arts college we had entered together after finishing our stint with the nuns, Hajira had bolted off to that dangerous institution that knew no barriers of gender, or worse, class: the Fine Arts College. FAC, as it was better known, was notorious in the public imaginary as the repository of all manner of obscenity and instigator of immoral behavior by "degenerate" artsy-fartsy faculty who supposedly threw lascivious pool parties (where?) to which they lured innocent, unsuspecting students and introduced them to drunken orgies and other such shameful *(tobah, tobah!)* yet obviously exciting *(tobah, tobah,* perish the thought!) behavioral phenomena utterly unknown and (virtually) unimaginable to the rest of us law-abiding, *shareef,* respectable middle-class Muslims. And sweet little Haji had entered this den of iniquity! How could her parents be so irresponsible? And worse yet, to let her have her way like this while they themselves were no longer in Lahore—Uncle Hashmi had been transferred as superintendent of hospitals—a big promotion for him—back to Quetta. So Haji had been left to her own devices—all that freedom, muttered our collective parental brood disapprovingly—under the much too lenient supervision of her divorced aunt, Safia Jehan, mother to the by-now also-divorced Izzi (that's why we never wanted you hanging out with him and other cousins of Hajira's, my parents now said smugly; I understood immediately that they had thus prevented him and "other male cousins"—each and every one of them—from marrying and divorcing me). So, the stage was now set for Hajira's fall from grace; we could only watch and wait.

When Haji introduced Sufi to gang of "cool" FAC guys and gals that had formed by then (of which I was an honorary member, even though I attended the stuck-up, all-girls' Kinnaird College all of them loved to

poke fun at)—he seemed harmless enough, though odd by our westernized standards. For one thing, he sported a beard, and not a discreet,
fashionable type but rather, an unkempt one that gave his already old-
looking, gaunt face an even older appearance, especially since there was
quite a bit of gray in it; in fact, because of it, he looked like a mullah, a
religious fanatic, a fundamentalist (funny I should think of this term
now—it certainly did not exist in the mid-'70s)—although he was anything but (according to Hajira, that is). The man was mild to the point of
being a washout; I mean, he was no Mr. Personality. In the presence of
guitar-playing, drop-dead gorgeous Jeeroo, joke-cracking, raven-haired
Machoo, and the delightfully talented and rambunctious Bizoo the
green-eyed dance fanatic (my favorite!), poor Sufi was what my teenage
daughter and her friends today would call a Loser (we weren't so mean
back then!).

He is wonderful, whispers Haji to me fiercely, don't you dare judge him
by appearance, Madame! I laugh and tease my best friend: don't tell me
you're falling for him, Shelley . . . she blushes and giggles, then, all serious,
turns those clear, trusting eyes on me and says, darling, don't call me that
name again, please. Seeing the puzzled hurt in my eyes, she reaches out to
touch me; we're not little girls anymore, Madame, those nicknames just
don't fit anymore. Then, grinning slyly: well, yours still does, Madame
Sin—but surely you can't imagine being called Sindy anymore, can you?
I see her point, and laughing together, we stroll off arm in arm, to grab
a coke and patty at the tuck-shop covered in the crimson bougainvillea
of early spring before we go our separate ways: she to her last class of the
day with her Sufi, they being the only students taking fine arts that year;
me to hail a rickshaw and head back alone to Kinnaird, where Mum will
be coming to pick me up in a half hour, hopefully none the wiser to my
playing hooky from a college I had by now become extremely bored with,

what with Haji no longer there; it was a good thing our B.A. final exams were around the corner—I could hardly wait to move on.

Haji and I turn twenty that year—1978—me in September, she in October—after a summer I spend visiting my parents in Dakar, Senegal, where my dad has been posted a year earlier. This is an exciting summer for me: it begins auspiciously, with the announcement in early June of the B.A. exam results; I have come in second in the nation. Pleased though I am at all the media attention—I make sure to give the newspapers my prettiest photograph—I am upset that the number 1 position has gone to our friend Honey. I now decide I had disliked her from the minute she'd walked in to class 9 in our convent and endeared herself to Haji, and later our whole inner gang, including dear old Hayley, Haji's older sister. I hated that she got to take that adventurous mountain vacation with Haji and her family, while I, who was her best friend, had to sweat it out in the sweltering heat of Lahore because my parents wouldn't let me go . . . *I hate them especially her Mommy dearest why does she never stick up for me I want to go oh pleasepleaseplease no is no but why? because of boys what boys she doesn't even have a brother it's what people will say after all a girl's reputation is all she's got we must safeguard you from all possible harm we are your guardians after all . . .*

Mummy and Daddy aren't around to share in my moment of fame and glory; Daddy has been in Dakar for over a year already and Mum left us to join him as soon as her college vacations started, taking Bholuboy with her but leaving Farhan, my youngest brother, and me behind to finish our postvacation extra-credit classes and exams in daily temperatures ranging between 105 and 110 degrees Fahrenheit with 100 percent humidity and fat ugly lizards crawling around everywhere.

We are children of the third world; we can handle anything . . . I smile and think of all the mischief I am going to get up to before getting on that plane to Cairo and thence to Dakar . . . it's time for a party and I am determined to host it in my parents' living room with the mustard-colored sofas and to hell with fat lizards. And so Bizoo and Sherry and Jeeroo and Machoo and Haji and her Sufi and God knows who else all arrive with crates of Seven-Up and Apple Sidra and guitars and tablas and we have to make do for the dancing portion of the evening with Deep Purple in the Rock and the Stylistics and Abba LPs playing scratchily on the pathetic radiogram that adorns the far left corner of the living room and rarely ever comes to life. Farhan has refused to join us . . . four years younger than me he is, but this is risky business; I mean, here's his sister, break-ing all the rules, having a dance party, a mixed dance party at the family residence, with the parents away; he knows they'd never have permitted such debauchery and so it's up to him to serve as male guardian of family honor. Sulking in his room is his way of condemning my behavior.

I feel lucky in retrospect—I wasn't whipped or imprisoned for cavorting with men to whom I wasn't related in the capacity of sister, wife, mother . . . a fate that has befallen many a woman since the so-called Islamic laws of Hudood curtailing women's rights in every arena were passed by the legislature during Zia-ul-Haq's military regime in the 1980s.

We laugh a good deal that night, and sing, and dance and chat end-lessly, downing those apple sidras as though they are contraband alcoholic beverages. We don't need anything other than our youth to feel drunk that night, though—and I am the drunkest of them all, laughing the loudest, high-fiving everyone every few minutes, being charming and witty and attentive . . . oh, I am the life and soul of the party . . . it's my party and I can cry if I want to, but I don't. I laugh instead, watching, watching Haji and her Sufi sitting cross-legged against the living room wall, shoulder to shoulder, eyes closed, lost in their own world holding hands. You are not allowed to do that, I want to scream, this is my parents' house and they would never approve. Around 1 A.M. she opens her eyes and looks at me dreamily, saying Madame this was a nice party but it's time for us to go (Us?)—and you should get these boys to go home too now. I thank her curtly for coming and respond, I can look after myself, thank you . . . the boys can stay as long as they want. We lock eyes for a second and then . . . she's gone, riding off into the early morning mist seated behind Sufi on his communist motorcycle. The party is over.

⟨∞⟩

"He is a communist," she says proudly, *"that means he is totally against this extravagant western capitalist lifestyle we've all adopted."* A year has gone by since that fateful party that got me grounded for the entire month I was in Dakar once my parents got wind of what I'd done (thanks to Farhan, the snitch, who told them, although I must admit, he did shoulder the "blame" for the party when my grandfather was informed of a "mixed" party on the premises by our cook, the other snitch. Farhan, to his credit, let Papa believe I was innocent—an image I desperately cultivated with my most beloved patriarch). I have been struggling to understand what's happened to Haji—to us—while adjusting to life as an MA student at Government College, my first "mixed-sex" institution. Her latest pronouncement leaves me feeling totally bewildered. Is this the Hajira I've known so well for the last nine years talking? "But . . . but," I stutter, "in spite of your name, you love to wear jeans and clingy T-shirts and listen to Leonard Cohen and Tchaikovsky and you inspired major envy in all of us after that marvelous hedonistic European vacation you took just a few years ago with your mum and sis . . ."

She shushes me with great ferocity. "Madame . . . that was all done under the influence of the western propaganda we've been victims of all our lives. It's cutting us off from our roots! It's turning the likes of you and me and that Bizoo you dote on into parasites, who prey on the lower classes of our wretched society." For the first time that I can recall, I am stunned into silence. I mean, to be thus accused by Haji is unsettling, to say the least—especially since she knows how strongly I feel about class oppression, how many discussions we've had over the years on the need to change the system . . . but not with this hateful rhetoric. And I observe, with a shock, that without my having noticed it because of my growing infatuation with Bizoo and simultaneous flirtation with the Rock (my classmate, Bakri, who, at six feet two inches and broad-chested like a tree trunk, is the complete antithesis of short, slim Biz), Hajira's appearance has undergone a change. Her perennially short hair has grown out considerably—enough so that she can pin it back to make it look more "eastern"—and she is wearing a shalwar kameez spun of coarse, home-spun cotton called *khaddar*—the poor person's cloth. And before I know it, she recites a poem she says she is ashamed not to have known all these years. It is a poem, she tells me, by our leading communist poet of the Urdu language, Faiz Ahmed Faiz.

> *Awr bhi dukh hain zamane mein muhabbat ke siwa*
> *Rahaten aur bhi hain wasl ki rahat ke siwa.*
> *Anginat sadiyon ke tarik bihimana tilism*
> *Resham-o-atlas-o-kamkhwab mein bunwae hue*
> *Ja-ba-ja bikte hue kucha-o-bazaar mein jism*
> *Khak mein lithre hue, khun mein nahae hue.*

She looks at me, triumphantly, knowing I am astonished at her newly acquired love of the Urdu language. She also knows I could not have understood much of what Faiz was saying, so she kindly launches into a translation for the benefit of colonized, elitist natives like myself:

> There are sorrows other than heartache,
> joys other than love's rapture.
> If there are spells of those dark, savage, countless centuries bodies
>   robed in silk, satin, and velvet
> then aren't there also bodies
> traded down streets and alleyways
> bodies smeared in dust, bathed in blood

bodies emerging from ovens of sickness
bodies with pus oozing from chronic sores?

I laugh and say, "Oh so let me get this: you and Sufi are not engaged in love's rapture, but some people-love thing, and you are connecting to their pain through Urdu poetry?" I look at her, daring her with my eyes. She is not smiling.

I shudder even though the sun is beating down relentlessly on Hajira, Sufi, Bakri, and me that day in June. Colleges and universities have been closed ever since April, when Zia-ul-Haq's army took over the government after Bhutto's party tried to commit election fraud. Bhutto has been thrown into jail, and while the nation awaits news of his fate, the army tightens its grip around our apathetic necks . . . Looking back now, I wonder at that apathy. Clearly, we had not absorbed Faiz's lesson at all. Here we were, the four of us, Haji, Sufi, Bakri, and I, meeting to discuss the trials and tribulations not of our country, under a martial law dictatorship for the third time in its thirty-year history, but that supremely silly thing called romantic love. Bakri has declared his undying love for me, mistaking my flirtation for something more than it is. Being Sufi's best friend, I know the three of them are planning to plead his case to me, and I am dreading the drama, for once. As I stand there squinting at the sun beating down on us in the compound of the American Center near Ganga Ram hospital, an oasis of imperial culture in the middle of a busy intersection of town, I am suddenly reminded of a day not so many years ago, 1974 I think it was, when Bhutto was at the height of his charismatic power and Pakistan was hosting the second summit meeting of the Organization of Islamic Countries.

I convince Haji to play truant from college—she is still with the rest of us at Kinnaird, this is before her fateful move to FAC—it is a glorious spring day, clear and quite warm actually, and Lahore is abuzz with the excitement of hosting the summit. "Haji, Haji," I whisper to her excitedly during Miss Barkat's psych class, "We have to go to Mian Salih's house in G.O.R—come on, we just have to . . ." and she, ever the studious one, glares back at me, shhhh. Miss Barkat, oblivious of anything but her own voice, drones on. "C'mon," I plead, "Gadhafi is staying there, and you know how I love him . . ." Even Haji cannot suppress a grin at my endless list of beloveds and she nods assent. As soon as class is over and before the bell for the next period rings, off we go, out the gates, into a passing rickshaw and then . . . here we are, right among the throngs of admirers waiting outside Mian Salih's compound walls for a glimpse of Gadhafi as his car exits the house. I am truly lucky that day, I have thrust myself into the front of the crowds, and somehow, somehow, when his car exits the gates, I find myself right alongside the vehicle, and ohmygod his window on my side is rolled down; I thrust my hand right into the car and feel his shoulder, military epaulets and all. When I get back to the college, I am in a daze, and all the girls want to kiss the hand that touched *him* . . . handsome Colonel Muammar Gadhafi of the Islamic Republic of Libya, a Muslim leader with socialist credentials, much like our own brilliant and dashing Zulfie Bhutto, who gave the mullahs a run for their money with his sophisticated defense of Islamic Socialism.

So how is it, I find myself wondering, as we four wait in the American Center's compound to have our student passes and bags checked before we can go in to its air-conditioned interior—that's why we picked it as a meeting place; we could at least count on being physically comfortable there, even though what we were gathered to discuss was, I knew, going to be painful. So, how is it that Bhutto, whom we all admired for walking out on the UN Security Council when those high and mighty powers tried to dictate the terms of our defeat in the 1971 war, how is it that he is now languishing in jail and we are here, thinking about love? "There are sorrows other than heartache," I want to say to my love-besotted friends.

It's the three of them against me, I think, my face and jaw setting into a hardness I know intimately. How could you, Hajira, I mean really, you've known me practically all my life . . . you know I'm a flirt, you know I string guys along, I don't mean anything serious by it . . . and here's this, this hulk, this silent giant who keeps staring at me and staring at me and just because I stared back you think it means I love him? Should love him? Are you all crazy? I hate, hatehatehate that Sufi, stupid smugface, his arm around Haji's shoulders claiming her for his own, why does he want me to be with Bakri? What's Bakri to him? I want to scream at him—why don't you go out on the streets and protest against the martial law that has thrown your man behind bars, the man who gave voice to your communist sentiments, his slogan of "roti, kapra aur makkan," bread, clothing, and shelter—a rallying cry for the poor and downtrodden masses you always claim to be fighting for? So I stand my ground against all that romantic moral pressure. I say no and Bakri weeps. I am disgusted by the sight of a big man weeping big tears out of his big big eyes. I turn on my heel on them all and walk out, tossing my hair back in my signature gesture. Strange coincidence that it is in America where I will meet my future husband and there that, twenty years later, will almost lose my marriage because of the man I left behind, flanked inside the American Center by my best friend and her husband-to-be. Betrayals never cease.

I know she has betrayed me; I feel it, and it hurts. But what scares me that summer is when I read Henry James's *Portrait of a Lady* for the first time, laying in bed in Dakar, forbidden to go out for yet some other infraction of parental law. Their punishment means nothing compared to the horror that dawns on me as I feverishly devour page after page of the disturbing novel. I recognize Gilbert Osmond instantly. I feel vindicated in my mistrust and dislike of Sufi. I want to warn Haji—he is no communist, he is after her money, her class pedigree—before it's too late and can hardly wait to get back to Lahore. And then it happens.

What I've been waiting for and dreading all my life arrives: the letter from Clark University, in Mas-sa-chu-ssetts. I can barely pronounce the name of the state that will become my home for the next six years of my life. I rush back to Lahore earlier than planned, to make all the necessary arrangements to leave for the United States of America.

I'm leavin' on a jet plane, don't know when I'll be back again, oh babe, I hate to go-o-o . . . my voice trails off in a bad imitation of John Denver as I try to remind Hajira of the songs we used to sing as teenagers. "Those were the days my friend, I thought they'd never end" . . . we're singing our theme song from that year at KC, the year we joined first year having completed our Senior Cambridge at the good old Convent of Jesus and Mary . . . Now it's Haji, Honey, Saira, Naumana, and Amena, Haji's older sister who has already become a part of our group; we're all sitting around a bonfire of notebooks from our last school year, but what was meant to be a merry display of youthful rebellion against the stuffiness of school has turned into something else. "Those were the days," somebody's voice cracks, I can't remember whose, but all of a sudden it's there: the memory of Sam, the last of our core group, recently, shockingly, dead. We look around at each other half-guiltily, ashamed at our merriment of a few moments ago. "Let's make a pact," I say, breaking the heavy silence, feeling the weight of five pairs of serious eyes upon me. "We'll never let that happen again. No man will do that to one of us . . ." The others nod in the deepening twilight as the notebooks turn to ashes.

It's hot, stiflingly so, even though it's the beginning of September. The heat, so oppressive with the post-monsoon-humidity still lingering in the air, makes planning, purchasing, and packing difficult. "Eheoow!" I scream as a pale-skinned lizard with a stubby tail darts out from behind some books I pull out of my bookshelf to take with me. "Thank God I won't have those to deal with in America," I say with no shame to Haji who is visiting and, having no such colonial squeamishness, just laughs at my reaction. I watch the lizard disappear into a crevice near the *roshandan* on the corner of my room's ceiling, and realize I'm going to be two weeks late to classes because the correspondence with Clark got delayed what with my being in Dakar, and I still have so much to do before I can jump on a jet plane away from lizards, mosquitoes, and roaches. . . . Anyhow, here I am, sitting in this damned hot room surrounded by twenty-one years of stuff—*bloody feels like a tandoori oven they say Fall is a lovely season*—"Haji, maybe you can come out next year and visit the leaves, I'm told, turn into amazing shades of gold and red and brown, even purple, your favorite color . . ." I trail off as she smiles at me dreamily, god I love that smile, and then she gets all serious again, that grim expression she's acquired ever since . . . I can hardly bring myself to say his name, but I must. "Haji, darling," I begin shakily, "I just want you to think, I know I don't have experience really, in the 'love' department, but, well, he is so very different, and, and" . . . now I feel myself getting shrill as I see her eyes glaze over . . . "class background does matter they say plus he's turned you off your friends and family; doesn't that strike you as—"

She silences me quickly at that. "Madame . . . listen carefully once and for all: I love him, and only when you fall in love will you understand how happy I am and how utterly wrong my parents and these societal values are that you're repeating to me like a parrot. I know what I'm doing—and sooner or later, you're all going to see how wrong you were about Sufi: he's truly a man of principle. He believes in living simply—and so do I. I spit on this bourgeois, decadent, westernized class we all come from . . . I embrace my roots now, and I am happy to give up material comfort in pursuit of a classless society . . ."

I am silenced. Attempting to laugh, I ask her, "I guess this means you won't be coming to visit me in the big bad west?"

She flashes that Sophia Loren smile at me for what turns out to be the last time, and giving me a big hug, says, "I love you Madame, I always shall, and I hope you find what you're looking for out there in America. But I've made my choice, and it is here, in this life, with Sufi and my painting. I hope you can understand and be happy for me." I hug her back. Mum knocks and enters, informing us that Haji's car has arrived to take her back to the college hostel where she's started living this year after moving out from under her khala's protective wing. She is doing here what I can only do by moving thousands of miles away. My mind races to unknown people and places as I wave goodbye to the girl who has been my best friend.

Before my first American academic year is over, I receive a phone call from the home I've left behind. It's Mum. She's crying, and repeating, "I'm so sorry, darling, so very sorry." She is sorry to have to tell me that Hajira is dead.

The bits and pieces I am able to put together on my next visit home to Lahore are, to me, surreal evidence of my prescience regarding Sufi the fake communist. I want to chase him to the ends of the earth and kill him, the bastard, murderer. Auntie and Uncle, and even Hayley who had shared some of my misgivings about Sufi (sweet Hayley, born again into Islam as a result of the loss of her baby sister), did not share my venomous anger toward the murderer of Hajira. "Madame, darling, we understand how you feel," *(no you don't! every nerve ending in me wants to scream)* "but while Sufi's behavior toward Haji was callous and insensitive, he did not kill her."

Oh my god. How can they be this way? "You've lost a daughter, a sister—all because of *him*—don't you see? Don't you want revenge? Do something! Do something! That son of a bitch walks free and Haji, talented, vivacious, sensitive, is gone. Forever. I want her back . . . he may not have pulled the trigger, but he had already killed her soul, her beautiful precious soul. He broke her heart and took her away from all of us, we could have helped . . ." I am sobbing uncontrollably, "he took her away from *me*."

"Sufi has put me in touch with my soul; I am so grateful to God for having brought him into my life" states an entry in Hajira's diary, a six-by-eight-inch ruler-lined notebook, a green paisley design gracing its cover. The entry is dated October 12, 1979, and I am grateful to her family for letting me look at it. That was the day of her twenty-first birthday, a month after I'd left for the States, and a week before her sudden marriage to Sufi, a simple affair held in her paternal aunt's home in Karachi. Karachi was picked because of its proximity to Sukhur, where Haji's parents had been living since their transfer from Quetta a few months earlier. In the photograph Hayley shares with me to bridge our separate griefs, Hajira looks beautiful in a paisley-bordered sari, green and gold, garlands of motia and roses adorning her hair pulled back in an elegant *joora*. Flowers are her only jewelry—none of the heavy gold bangles, necklaces, tikkas for the forehead and naths for the nose that typically weigh down the virgin bride. Her limpid eyes reflect a deep sadness she is unable to hide from the camera's uncaring gaze. Uncle Hashmi looks awfully stern, his chin with its Kirk Douglas dimple jutting out more than usual. He is not smiling. Auntie Sana, the mother of the bride, sits next to Haji, her arms around her, an expression of confusion and worry conveying itself through the strange half-smile hovering around her mouth; Sufi's mother, whom I had never met, stands behind her son, her hands grabbing his shoulders in a proprietary gesture. She is much more conservatively dressed than Haji's mother, who is wearing a sleeveless blouse with her sari while Sufi's mother is draped in a full-sleeved shalwar kameez, a large chador-like dupatta covering her head and ample bosom. Sufi is in the center of the photograph, self-effacingly dominant in his Lennon glasses and traditional white shalwar kurta, golden khusas the only concession to the frivolity of wedding-wear. He is the only one in the photograph who is smiling. Hayley, oddly wearing black, stares straight ahead with eyes wide open, as though she has just seen a ghost.

Haji's smile was the best expression of her soul—clear, and generous—and he took that away from her, remembers Auntie Sana sadly, holding my hand as I sob.

There is a hiatus in the diary entries till March 11, 1980, when a single phrase announces a startling fact: less than six months after her marriage, Hajira writes, as if noting a change in weather, "Yesterday, I became a mother." I am told by Auntie and Hayley on separate occasions, both times seated on a chintz-covered sofa worn out by years of use in the living room of the Hashmis' residence, that Hajira's slide into postpartum depression wasn't helped by her husband's long absences from home. The house, with its palatial gardens and sprawling interior, to which Uncle, Auntie, and their remaining daughter moved back after Haji's death to take over the care of the infant son she'd left behind, had been the house offered to the bride and groom as rent-free living quarters after their wedding. How interesting that Sufi, Mister Communist himself, "a man of principle" as Hajira had been led to believe in the first flush of their romance, who decried material comforts as signs of the decadent and morally corrupt bourgeois lifestyle of people of Hajira's family's social class, should have accepted so readily the comfortable goodies from the people he had denigrated and mocked in front of his wife-to-be.

Not only did he move without a second thought into the home of his despised in-laws, he got to work on Hajira to obtain a new car from them for his personal use. "They can afford it," I imagine him saying sneeringly. And then he would vanish. For days on end, and nights too, he would disappear, with nary a word of explanation to his recently wedded wife and mother of his newborn child. Apparently, these disappearances coincided with the culminating session of the master of fine arts degree program, the fateful program of study that had brought Sufi and

Hajira together four years prior. "He tells me not to be a nag, that I'm in danger of becoming a frightful bore," scrawls Hajira in spidery script, letters weakly formed in the wake of exhausting childbirth. "He tells me my work just isn't very good anymore, that I should simply let him be the artist in the family, and reserve my energies for the baby; perhaps he's right. I really don't want to bog him down, and I certainly have no desire to be in competition with him."

Hajira's parents are so fair-minded, I want to puke. They tell me that depression really is a difficult disease, a chemical condition that eludes the understanding of "normal," "healthy" folks, especially ones unschooled in the medical profession, such as Sufi's mother. She was called in to help with the household chores, especially with looking after baby Asif, a male replica of Hajira down to the hooked nose and the dimpled chin. Boy, how it must have irked her to be reminded of her grandson's weak lineage every time she fed, bathed, held him. In a rage at what she perceived as Hajira's self-indulgent "rich people's illness," she flushed her medicines down the toilet one fine afternoon, exhorting her daughter-in-law to resume her maternal duties, which included breast-feeding the baby boy—an activity that had to be halted while Hajira was on medication.

As Hajira withdrew more and more from the public sphere, shrinking deeper into a despair no one could or would enter, admitting to her diary, "I have made a terrible mistake, but there is no way out," Sufi's star began to shine ever more brightly. Her mood, I would like to think, reflected the mood of the nation, where that autumn Zulfie Bhutto was put to death, having refused offers delivered to him in prison through Zia's intermediaries to leave the country. "This is my country, why should I leave?" he is reputed to have said. Zia, angered by his intransigence, also realized that Bhutto remained a hero to the people, many thousands of them coming out in spontaneous protests all over the country in his support. No wonder he had him executed in a hurry one terrible night, in spite of pleas for clemency from leaders of the so-called free world pouring in. Sufi, once an ardent Bhutto supporter, did not, I am told, cry too many tears for his erstwhile hero's murder at the hands of the new establishment. He was too busy enjoying his newfound stardom as an artist, and who will blame the poor boy who has made it big? He was named the winner of the fine arts medal of honor, and many offers for commissioned works, including from places abroad, like Austria, flowed in. He became the life of the Lahori arts circuit, boozing and smoking fine cigarettes at every elite party in town. He became, our Sufi, a veritable man of the people!

Then, one day, the popular couple, or should I say the popular husband and his sad-eyed wife, got invited to dinner by the very hip, biracial artsy-fartsy couple who, by sheer coincidence, rented the upstairs flat of Hajira's maternal aunt's two-family house—the same house where Haji and her beloved Sufi used to meet for secret trysts during those early months of courtship. She sent her eight-month-old husband upstairs with their two-month-old baby son while she went to get something she claimed she'd forgotten in her khala's bedroom on a previous visit. Khala was out of town, but the house and her bedroom were open, her ancient, trusted cook and general housekeeper Bilal in charge of affairs while she was gone. Haji told Bilal to leave her alone to look for the misplaced item, and to go upstairs. *Tell Sufi sahib to come down here in a few minutes, okay? Tell him Hajira bibi has a surprise for him. It's his birthday today, and I had actually left his present here last time I came, so I could surprise him. Bas, ab jao, go now.* As Bilal turns to go, nodding, "Ji, bibi, as you say," Hajira says to him, softly, *Shukria; thank you for always being there. Tum achay aadmi ho.* Embarrassed, and somewhat confused by this sudden affirmation of his goodness, Bilal backs out of the room hurriedly. Haji smiles, her eyes dreamy in that way she had. Bilal does as he is told, and as he and Sufi come down the steps, they hear what sounds to them like a firecracker going off. Puzzled, possibly alarmed, they rush to the bedroom, and throwing open the door, they discover Hajira's body, lifeless, the gun still smoking in her right hand, blood oozing out of the right side of her temple, her mouth twisted in a sardonic smile.

I am told Sufi fainted when he saw the surprise his beloved wife had prepared for him.

3

Saira

She came to the party with bells on her ankles. Tiny silver peas tinkled ever so slightly every time she moved her creamy golden legs. We sensed rather than saw them behind the billowing cotton shalwar that draped but couldn't quite hide the curvy texture of her blossoming womanliness. The matching sleeveless kameez she wore served as a most appropriate figure-hugging device to balance the shapeless shalwar pants. And, amazingly, she wore no scarf-like dupatta. In my grandfather's drape-darkened drawing room, with its heavy oak furniture dating back to the days of the dinosaurs, Saira was a revelation. We gawked and gulped as only twelve-year-olds can, knowing our flat-chested, flat-bottomed bodies looked pitiful in comparison.

The party is a huge success. My friends tease me about staging my own farewell; you really should have let one of us do it, they say. But I'm afraid if I don't, no one else will, and I will be sad because the test of friendship will have failed and who wants that. No, no, much safer this way so when I go off to Nairobi I can carry memories of my own popularity with me and never feel alone or friendless in the Heart of Darkness. Never mind that good old Conrad wrote about the Congo in the 1890s and this was the 1970s, and I was off to Kenya not the Congo. Africa was an alien place, dripping with mystery both frightening and alluring to an almost-thirteen-year-old with an over-active imagination.

∽

Shamshad, old faithful, serves us lemon tarts and cream rolls, deep-fried samosas and ribbon sandwiches with tea and Coca-Cola, rolled in on my grandmother's fanciest carved wood-and-glass tea trolley. I really have to beg my ammi nani to let him do that; she doesn't understand why we can't simply get up and go to the adjoining dining room for tea and snacks like normal kids our age. "Want to play begum-sahibs, is it?" she laughs. "Wait until you have to be one for real, managing a house-hold and servants and having to put up with . . ." She trails off, finally relenting with a twinkle in her eyes, "Acha, baba, I'll have Shamshad bring in your tea and you can do the honors yourself—just try not to get crumbs and sticky paw prints everywhere, okay?"—which admoni-tion of course only succeeds in getting me all worked up and irritable, exclaiming, "Ammiji, my friends and I are not kids anymore, okay?" Suddenly, I can't wait to get to Nairobi and have Mum exclaim, "how grown-up you've become!" A lot can change in a year. It's only my ammi nani who seems oblivious.

The ribbon sandwiches have been prepared by Saira as a special treat; she knows how much I love them. They look so pretty, red-green-yellow, ketchup–mint chutney–egg salad, the edges trimmed off, very dainty indeed. Part of our colonial British heritage, I am sure. Perhaps that is why I love them so much, yet I cannot help rolling my eyes in between bites and muttering mockingly, "How ridiculous to spend so much time and energy prettifying food that is only going to end up in the potty . . . and you are so good at this sort of thing, aren't you Saira dear?" She isn't dumb, that Saira, despite what I refer to in friendly gossip snobbishly as her "Urdu-medium" upbringing; smiling sweetly, she replies, "Be careful, Madame"—short for Madame Sin, as I am already called by my friends, much to my chagrin—"don't pooh-pooh the art of food preparation so much, or you'll end up on the shelf, high and dry, while we bring you ribbon sandwiches from our oh-so-married households!"

Everyone laughs, though I feel compelled to have the last word: "Maybe some of us don't want to get married!" Now it is everyone else's turn to roll their eyes; "There she goes again," I can almost hear them sighing in unison; they insist that I open my presents. There are perfumes and lipsticks, which we giggle over as you would over contraband items; frilly notepaper embossed with violets to write home letters; some Barbara Cartland and Georgette Heyer novels to read on the plane journey to "the land of the darkies"; and a beautiful painting of sunflowers—my favorites—by Hajira, the budding painter among us. I open Saira's gift last. It is a beautifully wrapped silver locket, in the shape of a heart. Inside the left cover it says, "From S to F, September 11, 1970"; on the other side is engraved, in a very tiny print, the phrase, "Forget Me Not."

Blue skies beckon in faraway lands; the phrase becomes a refrain to shape a life of leave-takings I can't imagine yet. I do know I am embarrassed by such insistence of identity. I hurry through the good-byes, and kiss Saira as lightly as possible. It surprises me no end to wake up the next morning to the sound of tinkling bells. I come wide awake, but the only sound in my room is the tick-tock of the grandfather clock on the wall facing my bed. "Hurry up! Hurry up!" I hear Ammi nani yelling. "Time to get ready for the airport!"

⌘

It is spring in Lahore, and the year is 2001. Who'd have thunk it, here we are—some of us, anyway—having made it to the twenty-first century, but Lahori springtime feels much the same as it did when we were twelve. A season, then and now, to bask in the warmth of the early March sun in our lawns or verandahs, before the intolerable heat makes us forget we ever actually enjoyed the glare of the orb. The sun feels glorious on our backs—we're careful to turn our faces away from its glare, lest our already dark complexions get darker, gawd forbid! The girlish fragrance of gulab and chambeli and nargis escaping the flower beds so meticulously cared for by the army of gardeners my friend Naumana the Begum Sahib has at her disposal is enough to make a believer even of me, hardened cynic that I've become in my forty-two-year-old mind.

As the bearer rolls out the ubiquitous trolley laden with sweet and savory delicacies meant for a party of ten, not three, I am drawn to the freshly squeezed anar juice, the rich red of the pomegranate seeds squeezed to the very last delicious drop. Like Persephone, I too, traverse huge distances to connect the different parts of my psychic and emotional life, rent in half by that fateful decision twenty-odd years ago to get as far away as possible from Mummy. America seemed the right distance, though I suppose that like Marlow I could blame the *Heart of Darkness* for igniting the original Kurtz-like fantasies in my head. Having "done" Africa at a relatively young age, America seemed the appropriate grazing ground for an intrepid and daring female explorer.

"So where is Saira?"

"Umm . . . she did say she'd be late, the driver had to first pick up Rania from the university, and that girl of Saira's," Naumana rolls her eyes, "always keeps her mom waiting," focusing her dramatically kohl-lined eyes on me, "the way you used to keep Auntie waiting, Madame . . . remember?" I laughed at the memory of my little rebellions, this one in particular having the power to enrage Mom—Auntie to my friends—beyond all others: "Don't you EVER do that to me again, or or or. . . ." her orange-lipsticked mouth a-tremble, beads of perspiration glistening on the fine hair above her upper lip, her tight little bun coming undone at the nape. I'd fixate on the last hairpin wiggling its way to freedom . . . and there, that final angry toss of her head would release that poor little pin from its duty so that it could fly off and vanish mysteriously in the dust-laden air kicked up by hundreds of girls yelling "freedom" at the end of another regimented day with the nuns . . .

Nomi smiled a little wistfully at the sound of my laughter, grown ever throatier over the years. "Those were the days, weren't they? Who knew what was in store for us . . . Saira and I have certainly had more than our fair share of sorrows, Madame, and then of course, there was Hajira . . . taking her own life . . . and Sam's murder before then . . . but . . . but you, Madame," she turns to me, suddenly bright, "you've managed to have enough fun for all of us!" Our eyes meet as we raise our blood-red glasses in a silent salute to survival, and yes, perhaps even individual triumph . . .

Sing-song bells peal at the front door to announce Saira's arrival, finally, finally.

Since we don't gawk anymore—having reached the wisdom and maturity of middle age—I find more surreptitious ways to gauge the passage of time. A long, lingering hug—which I can tell is making her uncomfortable—and a few sidelong glances reveal more than I want to see—a body grown slack and shapeless under the finest pure silk shalwar kameez rupees can buy. The breasts that had so held me in awe on the verge of adolescence have turned into overripe watermelons, jiggling uncomfortably at every move she makes; you can see them heave even behind the large silk dupatta she wears modestly draped across her bosom. The rest of her outfit, like the dupatta, is meant to conceal more than reveal. The days of sleeveless, figure-hugging shalwar kameezes are over, I sadly conclude as we walk across the sprawling lawn to the covered verandah where a table and chairs have been set up for our lunch. "Honestly, Nomi," I exclaim, "how you can expect us—well, me at any rate, since Saira missed the trolley goodies—to eat again after all that, I don't know . . ."

To which they both reply, almost in unison, "You can afford it, Madame," and then we're laughing, transported back to feelings we can almost touch.

"Hey, you guys, I do have breasts now, ok?" I say, which fetches another round of cackles, although Naumana worries for a moment if the bearer could have heard . . ."Shhh . . . Madame . . . this is Pakistan . . . what if the bearer hears . . . speak in English . . ."

I am amused at her concern. "And you think he wouldn't know what 'breast' means? You can't be so naïve! What difference does it make?" and I can see them both rolling their eyes, "here she goes again," they're thinking, just like old times. . . .

But it isn't like old times after all. As we settle down for a few moments of shared intimacy after a delicious lunch of sizzling pooris dripping with ghee, golden halwa layered with almonds and raisins, seekh kebabs fresh off the grill, and my favorite, haleem—spicy lentils cooked with chunks of lamb and wheat smothered in fried onions and garlic—my sated palate slowly churns into a mess of nauseous rage.

It begins innocently enough. Saira has seen an earlier version of my story of her, and has, according to Nomi, been offended by it. I am incredulous. Pleased, touched, even flattered, those were the reactions I would have expected. But offended? By what? I turn to demand in genuine puzzlement, only to be met with a nervous giggle, most unlike the Saira I once knew. "Well, Madame Sin, what's with all those shameless references to my legs and bosom hunh? I do have grown girls now, you know, marriageable age . . . and what if my twenty-year-old son were to catch hold of that description? Tobah, tobah," she shudders, touching her ears with her fingers in the classic gesture forswearing unthinkable thoughts, while I sit back, dumbstruck by the thought that my artistic endeavors have been mistaken for pornography. Seeing the hurt on my face, Saira, ever perspicacious, laughingly teases, "You would be embarrassed too, Madame, if you had kept pace with us and been at the grandmotherly stage God had in store for you, instead of prancing around like a pretend-teenager ducking your destiny."

Now I am tickled, and in the spirit of tit for tat, shoot back, "Achhaji, really, seems more like you and Nomi have grown old before your time, and you just can't take a contemporary looking like she belongs to your kids' generation," at which there are further hoots of laughter, and I'm glad I'm exaggerating because the truth is, life *has* turned out differently for us. "You managed to escape, Madame, and it shows" is written all over their desiring, happysad faces . . .

The rest of our afternoon together depresses me as I realize my two best friends have become religious zealots in a way I could not have anticipated when we were giggly girls together, sighing over boys even if we didn't dare go further than fantasize about our romantic desires. The decades of the 1980s and '90s have truly changed the way people think, I sadly conclude. For despite the good-natured tit for tat between the two begum sahibs and me, the inveterate outsider, I realize I am no match for their newfound faith in Islam. "Madame," Nomi, turning her puppy-dog eyes on me, says at one point between cups of cardamom tea, "do you pray?" Mistaking my startled look as evidence of my guilt, she continues breathlessly, "You know, you really should. I have found so much peace in my life simply by turning to God and prayer, as we are enjoined to do five times a day by our prophet and the Quran. You should try it sometime; maybe," and here she smiles as she looks at Saira, "that will make you write different stories than ones in which you concentrate on our body parts!"

"And you, Saira," it is my turn now to act superior and sarcastic, "have you found religion too? Are you similarly comforted and peaceful in your old age?" Before she can respond—and she is a sharp one, even now—I quickly add, "Honestly, girls, how can you have become so influenced by this religious claptrap forced down everyone's throats by the last wretched dictator and his mullah henchmen?"

I am referring, of course, to General Zia, who had ousted the first democratically elected leader Pakistan had had since Liaqat Ali Khan was assassinated in 1959, the charismatic People's Party leader Z. A. Bhutto, in 1977 in an unconstitutional coup, then hanged him in 1979 shortly after I'd left for the USA. In the following decade, before the dictator himself met his violent end in an airplane explosion, he had declared himself Ameer-ul-Mumineen—Leader of the Believers—and installed a slew of fanatical mullahs in positions of power in the government and the media, like Dr. Israr Ahmed whose many virtues dear Nomi extolled now for my edification. "Madame Sin," she said to me sweetly, with extra stress on the "Sin," I thought, before Saira could get a word in edgewise. "These mullahs you are so quick to deride, especially Dr. Israr Ahmed—they are very educated, you know, and could teach people like you so enamored of all things western a thing or two—couldn't they, Saira?"

I can see this is turning into a battle for Saira's approval. "Well," she responds in her usual measured fashion, "it's true that all of us were raised without any real attention being paid to our developing a true understanding of the Quran . . . let me finish, Madame—" as I butt in exclaiming, "Are you guys telling me we were raised as anything other than Muslims?" She continues, calm as those cucumber sandwiches she brought to my party thirty-odd years ago, "While it's true that we have always been a Muslim society and yes, we all were taught to read the Quran in Arabic, yet we never really understood what we were reading."

I am incredulous at this turn in our conversation. "We were taught enough. And those of us who wanted to, read the Quran and even the hadith in English when we got older. Are you telling me that these perverted maulvis, with their sex-obsessed minds, if they can be credited with having minds . . ." I am sounding shrill even to myself now, but I can't help it. "What can these men have to teach us women about our desires, our rights, about what we can or cannot do? You of all women," and I look at Nomi accusingly, who turns away from me, knowing what

I am about to say, "you should know better than to trust these men. Your ex-husband was able to take your son away from you after he deserted you, and you cared for that boy for the first seven years of his life without a rupee from that bastard Yaqub. He never inquired after his son even once in all that time, and then—boom!"

I am appalled at my insensitivity as she turns her saucer-sized eyes back at me, this time looking at me unflinchingly as the tears threaten to spill over but don't. "Yes." Her voice is soft but firm. "It is true I suffered from the Shari'a laws that give the man, the father, the right to his offspring no matter what. But Madame, if that is God's will, we must accept. Who are we to question His infinite wisdom?"

I want to scream at her; this is not about God's will, it is male interpretation of the scriptures, but I desist in deference to her suffering, ashamed of reminding her of what she, I know, must try to forget every day of her life.

"Dr. Israr's lectures helped me come to grips with my life, my loss, Madame." She is almost pleading with me now. "Don't you see, we have to stop seeing everything only as it affects us individually. We must overcome these false divisions between what we see and feel and what is in fact, the real truth of existence. Madame, did you know that Dr. Israr is no ordinary maulvi? He wrote a significant tract in 1967 in which he explained his basic thought that an Islamic Renaissance is possible only by revitalizing the Iman"—true faith and certitude—"among the Muslims, particularly their intelligentsia. That would be us, Madame!" Once ignited, dear Nomi could be very passionate about communication.

I nod, and smile in spite of myself. It's funny to hear words like "intelligentsia" coming out of Naumana's mouth.

She fervently continues her sermon to me. "The revitalization of Iman is possible only by the propagation of the Quranic teachings and presenting the everlasting wisdom of the Book of Allah in contemporary idiom and at the highest level of scholarship. And this undertaking is essential in order to remove the dichotomy between modern physical and social sciences on the one hand and the knowledge revealed by Almighty Allah on the other. You know," she adds with great pride, "this tract is available in English as *Islamic Renaissance: The Real Task Ahead*. You should read it sometime. And isn't it praiseworthy that Dr. Israr Ahmed gave up a thriving medical practice in 1971 in order to launch a vigorous movement for the revival of Islam? As a result of his efforts, the Markazi Anjuman Khuddam-ul-Qur'an Lahore was established in 1972, Tanzeem-e-Islami was founded in 1975, and Tahreek-e-Khilafat Pakistan was launched in 1991."

I am stunned by this information gushing forth from Nomi's mouth. While Saira looks impressed, I am horrified. "Khilafat movement? In Pakistan? Are you serious?" Both my friends look at me smugly.

"What's wrong with that?" Nomi challenges.

What's wrong with that, I want to scream at them, is that you all are falling for a scary fundamentalism. What's wrong is that men like Dr. Ahmed, a pet of Zia-ul-Haq's illegitimate regime, is allowing this dictator to whitewash his regime by cloaking it in the garb of an Islamic government. The ultimate objective, of "establishing a true Islamic state" or Khilafah in Pakistan, will only come to pass at the expense of the rights of women, the poor, the religious minorities. All those who cannot defend themselves against charges of anti-Islamism, all who will be told, "cover up; listen to your menfolk; don't go outside your homes; don't acquire property; whatever you have belongs to your menfolk; be obedient wives, daughters, mothers; Christians and Shias and Ahmadis are blasphemers; let's kill them, burn their mosques and churches, get their properties; let's rape the poorest of poor women and accuse them of fornication and adultery, let's force young girls to marry men old enough to be their grandfathers, then cut off the noses of those who dare assert their desire to marry men their own age; let's cut off the hands of thieves no matter if they robbed to feed their starving kids; let's do this all in the name of reviving Islam. . . ." Yes. This is all that I want to scream out loud but don't.

Saira is getting married. She'll be turning eighteen the day after her wedding, and we are bummed because it means no lavish birthday party at her mom's house, and no flirtatious looks exchanged with her dashing older brother Shahid across the dining table laden with goodies. Hajira, Naumana, Amena, and Honey are all in love with Mr. Dreamboat, tall and fair and deliciously shy, peeking at us nervously through his horn-rimmed spectacles . . . that is the clincher, since we are all aspiring intellectuals. I am convinced it is me his thick-lashed eyes seek out from behind those sexy glasses, but I don't want to dash the others' hopes, so I say nothing, except smile smugly whenever his name is mentioned.

And then we all realize, almost simultaneously, that the wedding will afford more, not fewer, opportunities for clandestine exchanges of hot and heavy looks . . . maybe, maybe, we might even get to say a few words to each other. My mind races ahead feverishly; I'm thinking I'll run into him going up in the elevator to Saira's marital chambers at the Lahore Intercontinental Hotel, to help her put on her bridal makeup, and there, oh god, he'll be, and, and the door will close, with just the two of us enclosed in the narrow box that will get stuck somewhere between the third and fourth floors and then . . . but my mind doesn't dare go any further than that and here is Honey, snapping her fingers in front of my face. "Stop daydreaming, Madame . . . what's wrong with you girls . . . doesn't anyone think this marriage business is happening much too fast?"

I am ashamed for having slipped into the delirium of erotic fantasies at the expense of my friend's future. We all know her maternal aunt, who is to be her mother-in-law now, has pressured Saira's mom into hurrying along the marriage. Haroon is off to Australia as a medical intern and will need a wife to keep him on the straight and narrow among those foreigners. Ergo, Saira and marriage, with bride and groom aged eighteen and twenty-five years. While Honey's or Hajira's or my own parents are hardly the sorts to rush us into early marriages, we realize that many of our friends are not so lucky to have such "broad-minded" parents—as Nomi and Saira are apt to remind us three when we get to go out to dinner or the movies and they don't. Especially if there will be boys involved. I mean, it is incredible—and yet, sadly, the norm for many of the girls we know, even at a liberal college such as Kinnaird—that most of them, including Saira, are not allowed to meet even their own fiancés! Since she was betrothed to H—her first cousin, which I think is gross, but the culture at large doesn't—Saira has not been allowed to be in the same room alone with him—imagine! Accepting our own westernized thinking as natural, even superior, Hajira, Honey, and I pooh-pooh the norms by which our "other" friends live as old-fashioned, even barbaric.

So the four of us are relaxing under the shade of the giant weeping willows on the front lawn of Kinnaird College one perfect October afternoon after classes when Saira breaks the news to us. "Remember my cousin H-bhai?" She whispers his initial, followed by the appellation of "brother," almost a requisite when referring to an older male cousin.

I cock an eyebrow from my prone position, head resting comfortably in Nomi's lap. "Yes? What about your betrothed?" my voice tinged with sarcasm. Saira has been "engaged" to this cousin since childhood, something Hajira and Honey and I find both amusing and weird.

"Well," she hesitates, lowering her eyelids coyly; her refusal to rise to my bait can only mean one thing, so I hear myself groaning, "Oh no, you can't be serious!" Yup, it's as I had guessed; Saira is getting married. The date, she tells us, is set for early January, during our winter break; that way, she won't miss any classes, and can go back to college when they resume. "You see, you all were wrong about my khala. She wants me to continue my education." Saira says this proudly, her smooth skin, with its pale complexion that darkies like me envy with a passion, stretched tighter across her angular face. "This mess," she sighs ruefully, running her long, tapered fingers through her short, "boycut" hair, "I'll have to grow it out, so I can wear it in a bun or a plait under my gharara's veil." She is smiling now, envisioning herself as a glamorous bride, and we are, in spite of ourselves, swept along with the excitement of the moment . . . one of us, unbelievably, is on the verge of becoming a begum, with a husband, and a house, and servants all her own. . . .

I remember the anticipation of new clothes for the wedding, the ginger first-time applications of makeup, the frenzy of phone calls to arrange who was picking up whom for the monthlong singing and dancing "practices" we attended at Saira's parents' house to get "our side" ready for the *mehndi* the night before the actual wedding. How we sang those sad songs about daughters leaving their *babuls*, their doting fathers' homes, for the punishing unknown of the in-laws, reveling in the magic of adolescent fantasies without once paying attention to the morbidity of the lyrics; how we danced the *luddi*—girls in their circle, boys in theirs, eyes meeting shyly across the room—we clapped and we twirled and we snapped our fingers in perfect unison, glittering in our peacock finery and borrowed jewels, while Saira sat, demurely covered in a ten-yard-long red dupatta weighed down with gold embroidery. . . .

"I'm coming, I'm coming," I scream from my bedroom window as Hajira's driver honks away in our driveway . . . I rub off the garish red lipstick so that I can look more "natural" and grab the ridiculous handbag mom has lent me for the occasion. Hajira looks gorgeous in a turquoise sari, showing off her curvaceous figure to full advantage. Her Sophia Loren eyes are lined with kajal and are they smoldering! "Do I look all right?" I ask nervously for her appraisal; I really don't like this beige and silver "moonlight" fabric Mom has gotten me for the wedding-day outfit. The kameez has a deep U neckline, although as my friends never fail to remind me, there's nothing much to reveal there! The pants are bell-bottoms, they're the hottest craze, and if nothing else, I'll be outfitted in the latest fashion . . . Hajira looks me up and down as I get in and tells me I look "svelte." I murmur a thank-you and remind myself to look up the word in the dictionary when I get back.

When her aunts and cousins finally bring Saira out into the reception room at Hotel Intercontinental and seat her on the dais covered with rose petals and draped with chambeli garlands prepared especially for her and the bridegroom at the far end of the chandelier-lit room, I begin to feel nauseous. I can't tell whether it's the overwhelming scent of the flowers, or the rich, greasy food, or the people or the exhaustion and excitement of the past month, or what, but as I gaze at Saira in her purple wedding gharara embossed with gold and silver roses, the twelve sets of heavy gold jewelry adorning her neck, hands, ears, nose, and forehead, her head bent almost to her waist with the heavy gold-embroidered dupatta of organza draped over her beehive-coiffed head, H-bhai sitting next to her in his smart black achkan (the traditional long coat), with a starched white shalwar and golden pagri wrapped around his head, smiling at everyone . . . well, the scene is too much for me. Just as I hear everyone yelling my name to come join the bride's friends and female cousins for the custom of *jooti chupai*, I dash out of the room at top speed, leaving the others to pull off H-bhai's shoes and demand ransom for them. The bathroom is not a pretty sight when I am done.

So, what was it like? We all want to know the answer to the Big Mystery, which feels like a hangman's noose waiting to choke off its next victim; we wonder which one of us that will be. S-E-X, a concept almost too scary to be articulated in a word, let alone be experienced. We just cannot believe Saira has done . . . *it!* She is giggling in her trousseau finery, wearing a beautiful white silk *jora* covered in freshwater pearls, and still made up like a Madame Tussaud wax doll on this, her third day after marriage. We are visiting her at her bridal suite in her in-laws' home (where the smell of rotting chambeli flowers reminds me, inappropriately, of the mausoleums of Sufi saints), and where, unbeknownst to us at the time, she will live for the next fourteen years of her life, bearing three children in a row, the requisite first son followed by two fair daughters. She ought to have been one of the lucky ones, graced with that first male heir, but . . . I am getting ahead of myself.

So, on that sunny winter day of January 1975, Begum Saira expanded our knowledge of sexual matters beyond our wildest imaginations . . . She told us, quite unabashedly, that she realized she was madly in love with her husband when he made her hold on to the side of the bed and stick her tush into the air while he proceeded to do unnameable things from behind. Hajira, Honey, Naumana, and I screech "tobah, tobah," pulling our ears in mock shame, and leave the room many shades redder than when we had entered it, followed by Saira's cackles of laughter all the way to our waiting cars and drivers in the driveway.

It is the beginning of March 1987, and I am preparing for my Ph.D. orals in the little house in Hastings-on-the-Hudson that my husband of four years and I have bought in anticipation of "becoming a family." I am pregnant, full-term, with our first child, which, in my desire to prove my emancipation from the patriarchal ideology of my "traditional culture," I hope will be a girl-child (little did I realize that the modern American culture I was now so delighted to be a part of harbored the same ideological desires as the one I thought I had left behind). In between rereading Wharton's *Age of Innocence* and *Ethan Frome*—which reminded me awfully of contemporary Pakistani society—and various and sundry books on "Raising a Feminist Daughter" and "How to Create a Nonsexist Household," I received the news that Saira had suffered a nervous breakdown.

The details were not clear, but this much I learned: she had left to join her husband, H (she no longer referred to him incestuously as "bhai," thank God) in London, a year after he had gone there to prepare for his FRCP medical exams. It had taken him almost ten years after their marriage—all of which they spent in Lahore in his parent's home, Australia having proved a convenient mirage—to pass the basic board exams in Pakistan. He blamed his repeated failures on the distraction of "family life" since Saira had proceeded to have three children in quick succession, thoughtless wife that she was proving to be—and so his mommy dearest had sent him far away from hearth and home to study with full concentration and pass those wretched exams designed to intimidate foreigners and come back home, a Medical Man at last. Unfortunately, his attention somehow got diverted from his books to one of the nurses in training at his ward (a failure of concentration he was doomed to repeat ever after), and when Saira's mother-in-law got wind of it, she sent her daughter-in-law on the very next flight to London to rescue her beloved son from the clutches of the devilish white woman. Of course, this meant Saira could no longer be around to massage her thrice daily or attend to the needs of her very particular palate at breakfast, lunch, and dinner or to listen to her incessant whining about how she was ignored by her one and only son ever since he'd gotten married (never mind that he was in London where she herself had sent him away from the clutches of his wife and kids . . . clutches, clutches everywhere, oh what's a mother-in-law to do . . .).

Anyhow, off went poor Saira to London to do her wifely duty, but God knows what transpired there, for she ended up being admitted to the psychiatric unit of St. Matthews hospital in the East End for two months. After her release, she was taken back to Lahore, H in tow, who once again could blame the wife for having distracted him from his studies by having a breakdown, thus preventing him from passing his exams. 40,000 pounds sterling down the drain, his mother would wipe her eyes every time Honey or Naumana visited their friend, still sequestered in her bedroom for several months after her return. Nomi wrote me that while the mother-in-law, Saira's very own maternal aunt, bemoaned the loss of money, Saira herself lost forty pounds in two months and developed deep black circles under her eyes; her face looked like Mt. Vesuvius oozing with lava.

When I saw her many months later on a visit back with my nine-month-old baby girl, the lava was gone but the eruptions had left deep craters on her face, and the circles around her eyes looked as though the sockets had been gouged out with a butcher's knife. I chatted non-stop during that visit with her, of this and that and that and this, then went back to my mother's, handed her the baby, locked myself in my old bedroom still pink after all these years, and cried and cried till my still-lactating breasts became so engorged that I had to let my bawling infant daughter suckle, milking them dry, slowly, slowly. Eventually, the tears dried too, under express instruction from Mummy that I stop giving in to melancholia lest the cheerful disposition of my baby girl come under its baleful influence. "Get up, get up, dear daughter," Mum breezed in while I struggled to control both my sobbing and my baby. "Hurry up with the feeding . . . you take ages with everything . . . we really need to get to the tailor's before the shop closes, or you won't have the lovely new jora in time for your cousin's wedding . . . can you believe it, the lucky girl, barely seventeen and she's nabbed one of the richest, most eligible bachelors in Lahore . . ."

I hear the Azaan for Asar prayers. God is great. . . .

4

Blood and Girls

Lahore

It is the tenth of Ashura in the Christian year 1997, the day the frenzied mourning for Hussain's martyrdom fourteen centuries ago reaches its peak for Shia Muslims the world over. I am visiting "home"— Lahore—on a research trip funded by my adoptive land, the United States. Hajira is long since gone from this world, but her spirit of endless curiosity and tolerance—nay, love—for the Other has seeped into me over these intervening years until I find myself softening into the madness that only love can bring. And so it is that along with the mother of another childhood girlfriend, Chambeli aka Cheemi, I find myself in the middle of Shahalmi, the working-class inner sanctum of Lahori Shiadom, swept along in a tide of sweat, blood, and tears at four in the morning. "Behen-chod, madar-chod—arrey, arrey—don't you have mothers and sisters, you fucking sons of bitches—hai, hai," even the countercurses are couched in anti-female rhetoric. But tonight, or should I say early morning, as the city pulsates under cover of darkness, throbbing in passionate movement as if awaiting climax at the moment

This chapter appears courtesy of the Feminist Press and Women Unlimited. It was first published in the anthology *And the World Changed: Contemporary Stories by Pakistani Women*, ed. Muneeza Shamsie (Women Unlimited, 2005; Feminist Press, 2008).

when the sun's first rays would rend its black shroud, melting into the shrieks and moans and moans and shrieks coming at hoarse intervals from the crowds of mourners, men receiving the sacrament, letting the blood flow freely between their gashes in a strange reversal of roles . . . so it is that this morning, Aunty—Cheemi's still-beautiful mom—and I are objects of veneration, Zainabs to their Hussain. "Let the women pass . . . araam-say, bhai, yeh hamari behenain hain . . ." The clanging of knives on chains hook and tear manly flesh punctuated with hypnotic dirges sung in honor of Bibi Zainab.

Santa Maria, the Black Madonna, Holy Mother of Christ, Jesus, Jesus, ya Ali!, ya Ali! Ya Hussain, ya Hussain . . . [1]
Ode I see
Odyssey
when blood
curdles to
speckle the
skin's dis/ease
who can say
how deep the
mottled hue
Lies
in the underbelly
of the beast

1. In AD 661, Ali was murdered and his chief opponent, Muawiya, became caliph. It was the death of Ali that led to the great schism between Sunnis and Shias. Muawiya laid the foundation of family rule in Islam and he was later succeeded by his son, Yazid. But Ali's son Hussain refused to accept his legitimacy and fighting followed. Hussain and his followers were massacred in battle near Karbala in AD 680. The deaths of Ali and Hussain gave rise to the Shia characteristics of martyrdom and a sense of betrayal. Today, Shias all over the world commemorate the killing of Hussain with vast processions of mourning.

sacrificed
annually a rite
of passage
entering
the New Year
with tears and
screams of
self-flagellation
exotic blood of
beautiful boys
bursts through the
tears of mothers and
lovers deep
inside somewhere
lost
to this manly
ritual of
torture
on display.

Spain

July 5, 1999, crossing the border back into Spain—Pays Basque, to be exact—is an adventure. Zara and I are stopped by the guards in a performance of power that we counter with the actors' power of performance—turning on the female charm full throttle, keep the motor running, *behen-chod, ma di . . . yaar,* why are you cursing so much, fuck it, *merijaan,* it's your bad influence of yesteryear . . . yours and Mehboob's—all his fucking and swearing, holy mother of Jesus, how many women did he hump at UVA . . . fucking asshole, he's still at it, tits and asses await him at every port, while the wife-who-won't-give-him-any raises their kids back home in Lahore.

So then, finally, the guards are apologetic, all that show of male authority come to nought . . . *Amusez-vous bien avec Ay-meeng-way* . . . clever man-in-blue, at least he'd heard of the great man . . . I nod and wink and off we go, still in possession of our packets of Paki charas (courtesy of Mehboob) as our victory charms.

First stop, San Sebastian. As Zara drives around looking for the P sign, I am looking for signs of my own—the cathedral, for one. I head straight for it once we've emerged from the subterranean depths of the parking lot—it amazes me how efficiently Z is able to figure out the parking protocols of foreign cities, never mind navigating the always menacing traffic. While she smokes her sixth Marlboro Light of the day, having expressed her distaste for cathedrals and bullfights in the same raspy breath—I enter the hallowed hall, its cool darkness a welcome shroud in which to lay at rest a spirit in constant, exhausting flight . . . minutes later, that thought too goes the way of all other delusional fancies . . . spiraling up with the smoke of the Marlboro Lights. After downing, rather speedily, the ubiquitous café con leche available at every Spanish street corner, we take some obligatory snaps and are on our way to the high point of my pilgrimage: Pamplona, where the sun is setting on the eve of Hemingway's centennial and the start of seven days of unabashed libidinal energy unleashed in honor of the fiesta of San Fermin, that ever-so-saintly bishop of Pamplona.

Mixing It Up

Na ro Zainab, na ro . . . don't cry for your brother, martyred in the cause of a just faith—always just, of course, but no, there is no room for the questioning impulse—justly silenced when confronted with the sheer magic of the Sanfermines, where popular religion and bullfighting have come together, conjoined for centuries. I want to feel the madness, lose myself running the *encierra*, wear white at the bullfights and drink till I don't know my name chanting *Ya Ali! Ya Fatima! Ya Abbas!* Beat that breast, baby, skin on skin.

You have become exotic
to yourself
grinned the professor in the ponytail
peeking through the lenses

the diamond in my nose
glittered in the sun
my blonde streak
fittingly flamboyant

she's become
a damned liberal
living amongst them so long
the husband's rage
foam on his lips
spewing forth
frightening
venom

those freaks those shias
shiites to your friends
he sneers
wallowing in their blood
i was entranced
by the beautiful boys
singing their songs
moving me to frenzy

in that climactic moment
between life and death
when all I could hear was the
clanging of the chains

before the blood burst forth
splattering my white kameez
and i thought
so this is ecstasy

remembering the dead
remembering the martyred
excess of memory
surfeit of pain
camera in hand
i beat my breast
so this is what it means
to be a stranger to my s/kin

Sylvie, our Spanish hostess married to a rich sheikh of Abu Dhabi with a keen interest in falcon hunting—at whose stunning villa atop a cliff overlooking the Mediterranean we spend our first two nights in royal splendor—is horrified at my obsession with the corrida. As we six sit on her stone and brick terrace—me still dripping wet from the morning swim in her pool, all enjoying the dark Spanish coffee and bread with cheese to fortify us for the morning's sightseeing adventures—Sylvie asks me, "Do you know they make young boys run in front of the bulls, and so many die each year? And what about the bulls? Such cruelty to animals! I am campaigning to ban this primitive custom . . ." This is to the cheers of the other women, Zara, her two cousins Bano Apa and Kimi, and the fresh young thing Asifa Merchant (no relation to Ismail Merchant). I guess I'm lucky Z has agreed to drive me to Pamplona at all—300 miles—to honor an old friendship and mock my literary fetishism, she says. But don't dare talk to me about bulls now or ever, okay? Meanwhile, grateful though I am to have her road skills at my disposal, I can't help thinking, what a bunch of—well, women, excuse me—I'm surrounded with, now that I've discovered the machismo upon which my feminism is built.

❦

My mother is horrified when I announce my intention of spending the night running with the mourners in the inner city on the Shia holy night of Ashura. Do you realize how dangerous this is? People are killed every year! How can you be so enamored of something as uncivilized as self-mutilation in the name of religion? You can't go! Tell your husband (spitting venom in my face) to take responsibility for your behavior—what will we do with your kids if you're killed in those mobs? Are you mad? The hysterical reproach from Mother's Ava Gardner eyes is almost too much to bear, especially when she confides to me in what has suddenly become a very pragmatic, no-nonsense tone of voice that Shias are known to pollute the town's water supply following this primitive ritual with blood from their bodies . . . what, I ask myself, is a poor, rational Sunni to do? Especially when, sitting at the dining room table for lunch—rare since we usually eat more casually in the enclosed verandah—I look up to see the cook, Irfan, agreeing volubly with Mum. *"Haan ji, baji,"* his eyes big as saucers, "your mother is correct. Those Shias, they are doing shirq."

"What?" I ask, stunned at this revelation. What the servant and his mistress were both saying was that Shias were non-Muslims. I realized that the rot that had set in within the fabric of Pakistani society, deliberately cultivated by the military dictator Zia-ul-Haq and supported by the government of my adoptive country, had settled deep.[2] I feel the bile

2. Since 1980, more than 4,000 people have been killed in Shia-Sunni violence. In Pakistan, as in most Islamic countries, the differences between Sunni and Shia were initially confined to academic debate, and violent incidents were extremely rare. However, the situation took a dramatic turn in the early 1980s. The change in the regional environment and the emergence of a political, albeit violent, Islam introduced a new phenomenon of sectarianism to Pakistan. The Soviet invasion of Afghanistan brought funding from the United States and Saudi Arabia for (mostly Sunni) Islamic radical groups to fight against Kabul. The Islamic

rising as I almost scream at my mother and her cook. "You two are simply parroting the extremist, hate-filled ideas circulated by jihadi parties like this . . . this . . . what is it called . . ."

Mom looks at me across the long table with its pretty white tablecloth now besplattered with curry stains from my hasty ladling of alloo gosht onto my plate. "Are you thinking of Sipah-e-Sahaba, perchance?" Cool she is as the cucumbers on my salad plate.

"Yes," my decibel level rising, "you all should know this bloody Sunni extremist Sipah-e-Sahaba is funded by the Saudi government so it can increase its influence in our country and the region, and our wretched dictator is helping them so he can stay in power with all this chaos and sectarianism allowing him to create his Islamist counter to keep pro-democracy forces at bay." I can feel the spittle forming at the corners of my own mouth.

"Hai, hai, baji ji, ki galaan kar dey ho," butts in Irfan the cook. "Damn, but he is a good cook," I think, enjoying the lamb and potato curry even as I am engulfed in anger and sadness at the state we have come to in this country, Muslim against Muslim. "This is no Saudi conspiracy, baji. Shias are the feudal lords in the district my family is from.

---

revolution that ended the monarchy in Shia Iran ushered in a new wave of Shia radicalism in the region. And when the Pakistani military ruler General Zia-ul-Haq tried to introduce his own concept of Sunni Islam to the country, a bloody conflict broke out.

Radical groups like Sipah-e-Sahaba and Tehrik-e-Jafria have their roots in the policies of those days. Differences between the majority Sunni and minority Shia Muslims date back to the very earliest days of Islam. They are directly linked to the issue of succession following the death of Prophet Muhammad. The Shia believe that after Muhammad's death, his son-in-law Ali should have been given the reins of administration. They still regard him as the first imam or spiritual leader. The Sunni, however, believe that the appointment of one of the Prophet's companions, Abu Bakr, as the first caliph was appropriate. The Sunnis also respect Ali as the fourth caliph of Islam (Zaffar Abbas, "Pakistan's Schisms Spill into Present," BBC, http://news.bbc.co.uk/1/hi/world/south_asia/3724082.stm).

Have you ever been to Jhang?" I shake my head, no. "You would see there how influential they are, how they squeeze the rest of us Sunni peasants, we who are in the majority."

Mum sits there, looking triumphant. "What would she know, this daughter of mine, who just mouths U.S. propaganda at us all the time? She doesn't know the realities of our country and the real reasons behind this Shia-Sunni conflict. Just like the damned Mohajirs of Karachi, these Shias are way out of control, having all the influence and claiming to be scapegoated all the time. Power brokers pretending to be victims . . . they all need to be put in their place . . ." she trails off, her eye caught by the clock.

"But, but," I splutter, "do you, of all people, so educated and with friends of all backgrounds and ethnicities, do you really think the Sipah-e-Sahaba's and Lashkar-e-Jhangvi's lobbying to have the Shias declared non-Muslims and calling for a ban on Muharram processions is going to help this country, help curb . . . ?" "Why are you so full of hate, so prejudiced?" is what I really want to ask her, but she has risen from the table. "Oh ho, you have made me late for your father. I need to run now and go pick him up." Ever the pragmatic manager, upset she is late for one of her to-do items for the day. End of conversation. I am suddenly no longer hungry. And tears won't come. (*Na ro, Zainab, na ro* . . . don't cry, Zainab, don't cry . . . Oh sister of the martyrs Hassan and Hussain, please don't cry . . . so goes one of the most popular dirges sung at Muharram processions. . . .)

> This is a pragmatic poem
> about a pragmatic woman
> my m/other
>
> she teaches me
> never to be free

of surfaces
smooth
      sailing

like a pumice stone
on my sole
rough skin sloughs off
as it appears

the seams mustn't show
this is Morrison's art
and mummy lives a/part
      so well

down syndrome baby and all
never upset her
nor daddy's tumor
and subsequent disfigurement

You came, then You left
accuses the supplicant
Look at my passport
no entries no departures
i was home
tending to my babies

she said
it is common to
hallucinate
after a major operation

I had bad dreams
as a child

bad men
rough bearded
breaking open our
house

my heart bleeding
something awful
as mother's led away
beautiful and elegant
in a white cotton
saree
jasmine in her hair

She looks over her
shoulder
with those Ava Gardner
eyes
as if to say
                it's okay

II
So I see her
with that man
purring sleekly
like a cat
his whiskers dipped
in mother's milk

it seems ages
have gone by
then I hear her
banging on the door
hysteria masked

practically
> underground

you didn't see anything
there was nothing
to see
now i must go and
pick up your
da-ddy

Sex, Bulls, and Shia Martyrdom

The night is young and warm still at 10:30 P.M.; it is summer in Spain, after all. The big ball of fire had barely disappeared as my girlfriend and I stepped lively out of our hotel in the central square of Pamplona, confronted immediately with the odors of human and canine flesh all mixed up with the pretense of perfumes unable to mask the peculiar aroma of rich, raw sex . . . sex was definitely, unmistakeably, in the air, pungent as an onion . . .

without warning the crowd gave way and the choked-up lane that couldn't possibly go anywhere opened into the mise-en-scène of a passion play. My eyes locked onto handsome uncle-by-default, Cheemi's oh-so-dashing air force wing commander mamujaan, intensely focused on the ritual unfolding in front of his stiff white kurta pajama, and, reassured, I slipped into the trance of the men, elbowing my way into their wavelength, banging, hammering, wanting to be let into the magical performance (for my husband the engineer, the hinted orgasmic state in hindsight is yet another in an endless series of betrayals, deserving only a venomous spit I must accept both outside and in . . .) fair flesh, dark flesh, thin flesh, fat flesh, young flesh, old flesh, hairy flesh, smooth flesh, taut flesh, sagging bellies, pounds and pounds of masculine meat so near and yet so far, I want to put my hands down under the skin beaten raw and red so the haze spreads across the broad manly chests and the boyish ones, I want to take I want to take I want to take my fingers and dip them deep inside the red-hot liquid and sign my name in blood Fawzia was here . . .

I see him on St. Nicholas Street first, then later inside one of those bars we danced and drank in, and I kept thinking *hai allah*, I hope he isn't a Paki, what will he make of the two of us hard-drinking Muslim girls (okay, okay, so we're both forty-plus, one rather stocky and short, the other tall and struggling against middle-age spread), and would you believe it, here comes another one, same doleful eyes, older, pockmarked face that make him look like Om Puri playing the fanatic's father in this year's hot new Hanif Qureshi film . . . I wonder if they are father and son, selling flowers to pretty ladies or perhaps to men in search of some.

I see him again, later—much later, a fish without water in a place with so much to drink, silently silhouetted against the pane of glass made hazy with so much heavy breathing. Tallish, but not too much. Slightly built, like someone not given to rich fatty foods, or to drink either. And then I laughed at myself. Why, of course not, he couldn't, he has only flowers, red roses at that . . . or perhaps, now waxing lyrical, that is a great deal to have, who needs food and wine? Still, he is an uneasy reminder—of what exactly I couldn't say—rather, unaware of my—our—existence, it seems; though the smile that wasn't quite one flits about the corners of his lips. I can see those lips even in the darkness of the bar . . . white shirt open at the neck, black pants hanging loosely on bony hips, a bunch of red roses, and sleek black—and I mean *black*—hair, falling, falling, and oh my god, are those . . . *chappals*? Why yes, indeed, open-toed, scissor-style—I never did like them, so typical of Urdu-wallahs I'd always joined my friends in mocking (poetic justice that I ended up marrying one, perhaps to assuage my own ethnic guilt). Through the mist I see him and then I don't. He is gone. Just like that. I could have sworn I saw him again, from the balcony of my hotel room where Z drags me back, unwillingly exhausted, at 3 in the morning. I go to hang my dripping bra and panties out on the railing above the bull-run path, and there he is, red, white, and black, turning the corner, just ever so slightly out of reach . . .

She was a very strange woman. So strange that they called her Madame Sin, not knowing what else to trace her infernal energy to. But that was in the before days . . . when evil consisted of setting fire to a poor bastard's peanut fields without really meaning to, and the thrill of the chase was a black man racing behind us kids with a scythe in his powerful arms, and danger was climbing into jamun-heavy trees, pregnant with plump, purple fruit, afraid Papa would wake up and discover us gone, and who would be blamed, the leader of the pack, Madame Sin herself, tearing around, even in the scorching heat of a 120-degree Lahore afternoon, or disturbing the peace on the outskirts of Dakar, in a little enclave of erstwhile colonizers. The thirst for adventure, even then, was unquenchable . . . why did her friends call her Madame Sin?

I do not know him yet, but can feel his interest, his passion for detail, his reporter's eye watching it all, drinking it in. A dark-complexioned man, slightly pockmarked, with straight dark hair that keeps falling into his face, making me want to clip it back. The tonga ride back to Aunty's home on Temple Road where we would try and sleep for a few hours before heading back at dawn, just before Fajr prayers, is incomparable to anything else I've ever done. It doesn't remind me of anything except itself. The byways and alleyways brimming over with perspiring hordes even late into the night are, finally, deserted, except for the odd mangy dog or cat. Clip-hoppity-clop go the horse's hooves, poor beast of burden, no rest for you, not tonight . . . Sahir blowing smoke rings while I scanned the sky above me for a sign of light, a little silver moonbeam to add the right touch to the surroundings, something to remember. Then, suddenly, there we were, at the old house peopled with our girlish laughter from convent days, oddly silent now . . . and that's when the spell is broken. No money for the tonga wallah. The reporter's jaib has been cut, the no-longer-so-stiff white kurta has a big gaping hole, wallet gone. What is he going to tell his brand new wife waiting expectantly for the first-of-the-month delivery? Lost the money running with the *portateri* alongside Madame Sin . . . ?

Girlfriend Where Art Thou?

The drive to D.C. is painful. I mean, the heat and the traffic, lordy lord, enough to drive a saint crazy, and being merely a sinner, I arrive at Cheemi's in a state of barely suppressed rage. Poor kids, they had to endure the brunt of Mama's anger, although, come to think of it, they're probably used to it by now, since just about anything and everything ticks their mama off (last night my husband said he might be forced to leave, he couldn't stand the rage anymore, festering festering, like storm clouds looming threateningly on the horizon . . . I'm scared, he said, poor Ju-Ju, and I, secure in the knowledge of a permanent love I mistrusted, made purring noises, meant to be comforting, which somehow came out sounding insincere, even to my prejudiced-in-favor-of-self ears).

Anyhow, where was I . . . ah yes, my friend Chambeli, a flower to me . . . well, it isn't exactly her house, not in the same way that the Lahore house had been hers, just as the residence at Temple Road is indelibly marked as her mother's place now that her father is gone. Cheemi's house in G.O.R., despite Mashuq's presence, really was hers, quite without a doubt. From the fragrance of the chambeli flowers adorning both front and back lawns, to the gold-filigreed cushion covers against ornately carved chair backs, to, of course, the signs and sounds of music everywhere . . . and that is the first thing I notice as I walk into the spotlessly white-walled, white-carpeted duplex on Windmill Court—her organ, on its stand, black keys in stark relief against the all-white background. Thank God some signs of her past life have made it into the new world she has entered of her own free will, emancipated woman that she is.

Hai, hai, do you know, she had that affair going all those years . . . haan, haan, bhai, I'm telling you na yaar, she's married that Richard Gere of hers . . . this is what those gossipy voices are whispering all over Lahore after she's run off to America, leaving Mashuq and her two teenage daughters and twelve-year-old son behind. My husband always marvels at the fact that all my family—and, it would seem, the fantasy lovers of my near and dear ones too—resemble Hollywood stars, all white ones at that: Wahid Mamoon is Gregory Peck, Mum's Ava Gardner, Dad, despite his facial paralysis, is, who else, Clint Eastwood, and Farhan, my brother, looks just like John Travolta especially after he shaved off his terroristic moustache. So it is disturbing that there are so many tears, at each and every reminder of the way things were, maybe the sense of loss (*quel gaspillage!* sobbed the insensitive husband one couldn't help feeling bad for, at the end of *Entre Nous,* one of my all-time favorite movies, when his wife finally divorces him and sets up house with her shell-shocked girlfriend); cultural and familial pressures are harder to endure than my friend had imagined.

I sing and drink a great deal, each sip of Bailey's Irish Cream, each note of Raga Malkauns, each silly little jingle of an Indian film song transforming into droplets of memory's perspiration, leaking out of the pores of our bodies and souls, our most blessedly confused happy-sad selves, skin resting on skin, salty tears and beads of sweat mixing with the peals of girlish laughter gigglygalote . . . and white-haired, white-bearded Richard Gere himself, playing quite the knight in shining armor, clearly chagrined by his perceived betrayal of King Arthur, nevertheless sits down to meals served by his Guinevere. I am nonplussed to see her playing this role, I must confess . . . and yet . . . when I sing again that night, David the son-in-law strumming away on his electric guitar in passionate accompaniment, it comes to me in the darkness of Darbari that Khayyam had gotten something right: nor all thy tears nor words will e'er erase a word of it.

The drive home to New York is a real drag.

Motherhood Is a Drag

Monday morning I scream and shout the kids into submission, and when I finally arrive at the doctor's office, she wants to know if my wearing red means something. I tell her I've just recently returned from Spain, where bulls and blood had taken over my consciousness. She tells me to get that kitchen done and stay home for the next few years. "Your teenage daughter needs you to stop running with the bulls," she advises, wagging the proverbial finger at me. "But I haven't really done that yet," I begin to protest, silenced suddenly by an image of Chambeli wearing red, twenty-two years ago. Haji and I are the only friends from school who make it to her wedding to a Sunni man, angrily shunned by her father. She is the first—no second, right after Saira—of our intimate circle to get married, exactly nine months after the Bengali has shamed her into a silence I still cannot penetrate, lacking, perhaps, the ability to love that way.

I could have sworn I felt Bakri's, the Rock's, eyes on me, boring through my rib cage at the precise moment when the matador locked his bull in a gaze to die for and plunged the sword deep, deep into the enraged beast's wildly thumping heart, silencing it forever. Greek Tragedy in Government College, Lahore, this is not, though neither is it the quick, graceful movement Hemingway had so admired. No, this is agonizing to watch. The bull writhes in misery, spurting blood and foam from its mouth, fixing its gaze on the lover's intent being who resorts to a second thrust, after which the creature continues to shudder convulsively for what seems an eternity, until finally all movement ceases and the eyes glaze over. Needless to say, the matador does not get his ear to toss into the adoring hands of the most beautiful woman in the crowd. Her disappointment is almost too much to bear.

There you stand
on those steps
on that hot summer's day
Such a dream come true
Ghalib's saqi, my muse

With a toss of your head
and a swing of your hips
how you hiss, stomping off
oh my love
sweet young love

what's the matter with you
has the cat got your tongue?

I wished then that the earth
would swallow me whole
chador, beard, passion
All

I'd rather *be* Ghalib
and/not his damned saqi
Writing those poems
yes inspiring those rhyme schemes

I don't want to give up
my power you see
so I'll be my own
slave, thank you, pretty please

but remember
dear departed
there always shall be
that question to consider
when our souls clash again

what shall we both do
having written our ghazals
always already
so hopeless, so silly
Imagining Forever
being Mad about Me.

5

Mad/medea

Prologue: The Kiss

What is it about traveling to foreign places and inhabiting other spaces that is so alluring to those who can't sit still but must keep forever moving, jumping on and off trains, buses, planes, breathing in takeoff anxiety, breathing out yes, I made it, I'm gone, off, away, this time to a chateau deep in the heart of la Suisse with Lac Leman glittering in the distance, atop a hill on a plain full of grape vines and cherry trees bursting with summer fruit ripe enough to lock lips with . . . what an embrace, passionate yet satisfying enough to make me say no to the *puis-je te voir encore?* coming out of the tree limbs I have climbed up my first afternoon there. How stupid to think one can prolong a moment.

The wind is smacking its scratchy kisses all over my body as it whistles and blows for the second of three days, rattling the white-curtained French windows so loud we think they'll shatter like fragile wineglasses. "After the third day it must die, it's the nature of the *bise*," pronounces Sophie reassuringly, with a smiling authority in her French-accented English. She is a native of these parts and will be the caretaker for a motley crew of writers, all six of us working on our masterpieces over the next three weeks of July 2005. Our first dinner conversation the night before had been about cancer and heart disease, agonizing decisions about whether to have that wine or forego the coffee instead, go for seconds on that delicious entrée with crème béchamel or hold back, resist; but the real conversation had been about men lurking in cherry trees and Scheherazade telling tall tales to the man who is her master so that she can live, another day, another moment. Was that clever, as most readers believe, or stupid? I could have told her what I meant to tell the man in the tree; no one lives forever, whether you feed on stories or cherries.

Another year, another season, in Cairo one late December evening, I sit facing windows opening onto the balmy night air softly billowing off the Nile, downing scotch, which I hate, hoping the writing might channel itself via my romanticized imitation of Hemingway. Odd that I would attempt such an impersonation in an apartment adorned by pictures of a very young and stunning-looking Nawal, exuding her fierce brand of sexual power as only a woman without a clitoris can do. *Women Without Men* notwithstanding, bulls and blood haunt my mind, so when I arrive at the chateau in la Suisse and am shown to the room marked "Hemingway" and told it will be mine for the duration of my stay—not Camus, not Nabokov, but Hemingway—and then later that afternoon when I discover a rusting steel bull with a horn broken off its head lying on the grass in front of its hoof, well then, I think, this has to be a portent. I must be meant to follow in the great writer's footsteps! Except, you see, I don't want to end up as a rusting one-horned bull in somebody else's garden . . . even a garden that grew as hardy a plant as my friend Madina, Maddy, Mad/medea. . . . she with passions that could kill . . . or like the character Firdaus in Nawal's novel I so admire, for growing even in a garden of filth, degradation, and poverty . . . nor do I want to be a flower in a garden celebrating the life of a writer whose machismo provides the courage I need to fly from home and back again . . . to kiss the lives and loves and cherry trees I want to hold onto but can't . . .

The cherry trees in Mad's mother's back garden in Lahore were not exactly cherry trees; they were, one could say, the Paki version of cherry trees, that is, cherry-like fruit with pits in it that you had to climb into the tree to get into your mouth. The orbs were plumper and more elongated and the flesh purple, not dark red, although blood stains after they've dried can be jamun stains or cherry stains, take your pick. And Mad always did look like she had blood on her mind; she was ready to beat the living daylights out of any man or woman, girl or boy, animal or human, older or younger, fatter or thinner, bigger or smaller—who dared say or do anything she perceived as taking advantage of her. You really couldn't bullshit her, not then, not now; why, that's as unlikely as a middle-aged Pakistani woman climbing up a Swiss tree to be fed cherries by a man she's never met before . . .

The Loo gives me no respite that afternoon in June. Lahori heat is like the passion I will know later . . . unremitting, *sans remords*, in its exacting, exhausting demands upon my body, my soul, and most importantly, my mind. Yes, the Loo, like the *Bise*, does not just kiss my skin's surface, oh no, it scratches deep into the dermis of my thoughts, drenching them in sweat so all I can do is lie there, all aquiver, waiting for the power outage that will surely come, yes, from an excess of energy and the heat it generates . . . impossible to sustain for long . . . yet here we are, here I am, waiting for the fans to stop whirring and then . . . that's my signal to jump out of the sweat-drenched bed and race over to Mad's, as if running at top speed down the road could prevent the sun from roasting me to a crisp . . . and then, up up, up the jamun tree in the sinewy silence of its welcome shade, there to sit in the broad pit of its stomach, contemplating the taste of purple rain in my mouth. I stick my tongue out and laugh when Mad appears at the bottom of the tree, commanding me to throw down the fattest, juiciest jamuns to her . . . she is too lazy to climb up and get them.

She completely overshadowed that poor Masroor, her maddeningly sweet and sour Viola larger in every way than his sappy Sebastian. I'm bigger than you, her movements taunted him, conveying more than the flowery gibberish that was Shakespeare to our ears, our very own Sheikh Piru. We went only to see the hilarious spectacle of a boy dressed up as a girl, or perhaps we went to see a more truthful masquerade, Madina the fresh-faced sixteen-year-old daughter of a six foot five inch, fair-skinned Pathan alpha male and African-born firebrand mother of Indian origin and darker hue, Madina playacting as the man she could have been. . . . Or perhaps we went because we could get permission for the outing; it was, after all, an elite affair on the lawns behind the Punjab Club, *Twelfth Night* by the Omega Players, a new English-language theater company launched in Lahore of the 1960s by Farhat Nishat Azin, or Apa Farhat as she was fondly known by those close to her and even by those not . . . Big sister Farhat, generous of girth and spirit, freshly dead, I hear, as I go flying off again to perch for a moment on distant blood-red trees whose fruit stains my pastel pink pants, like age spots on a brown complexion, not there when I last looked, now impossible to scrub off.

And so. I think perhaps Madina will always be Viola in my mind, an image of fresh-faced violence, an innocently masked fury lurking not too far from the surface, ready to unleash a volley of abuse at unsuspecting rickshaw drivers and best friends alike. No one could accuse her of discrimination! *Teri ma, behn aik kar diyaaan gi, behenchod, madarchod*, you sister-fucker, what, do you think you can charge me 20 rupees for a ride from the college to my friend's house in Chowni? Ki samjhiya ai meinoon? I'm no fool, okay, I know you people, always trying to take advantage of poor innocent girls like me . . . get out out, before I call for the police or my brother to beat the shit out of you, or my friend Fawzia here, she'll bring her servants, her brother out in a minute. . . .

I'm appalled, ohmygod, why did I agree to take the rickshaw ride with her back home from college, me, her star-struck junior, freshly in love with her Ariel in yet another Sheik Piru production, this time on the stage of the most famous girls' college in Lahore. I want to shrivel up, become a mango skin she could slip and break her pretty neck on, anything to stop these terrible words flying out of her mouth at breakneck speed, I mean I've never even heard some of these terms . . . sister-fucker? Sweet Jesus, what would the nuns at the convent we both attended before college think if they ever heard the captain of Unity House carrying on this way? Is she quite mad, I think, she can't be serious about my going in to call my servants or brother to get mixed up in this low-class brawl; what if the servants really did come out, holy Moses, I'd be in deep doo-doo . . . I mean what if my elderly aunt stuck her head out her window at this very minute? I'd be blamed for causing her a heart attack! Worser and worser, what if Mummy came back and heard all this ruckus and me in Mad's unsalutary company (I'd been warned several times of the ill effects on my girlish reputation should I continue in my dazed pursuit of her). Oh dear, oh dear, and she'd know I'd gotten back home on a rickshaw without her maternal permission . . .

Just as I'm about to collapse under the weight of the what-ifs and thoughts of ensuing punishments, the volley of curses stops. "Here, take these ten rupees," gruffly warm now, "be a good boy" (boy? The man is old enough to be her grandfather!)—"shabash, yes, go get yourself something to eat and drink, it's a hot day, you look tired, go on now. . . ." Smiling sweetly, Viola's back again, and she's ravenous for those fried pakoras stuffed with onions and chili peppers she can smell being fried in our kitchen for afternoon tea. I smile weakly at her as she grabs my arm and says, "We deserve something tasty after that, don't we? Aren't you glad I saved you ten rupees?" I stagger up the steps to the side door of the house, suddenly exhausted, and yes, quite famished. Those pakoras do smell great, nodding agreement with Maddy, as usual, who looks flushed after her most recent performance. We go in, and I find myself thinking fleetingly of the rickshaw driver and how his lower lip quivered wanly as he faced the torrent of Mad. A skinny man with a white day-old stubble on his face, he looked like he could have used some pakoras too. Madina ate a plateful, then another, while my cook gestured to me that he didn't have any more prepared. I wondered what I'd say to Mom when she got home for tea without pakoras.

☙

Madina's father is dead. He has always been dead, for as long as I've known her, and of her. I have often wondered how he could have allowed himself to marry an outsider, a woman like Fallahat, so plain by Pakistani standards, dark and thick-featured, and a writer to boot! And not just any writer, but a real Marxist, a woman whose experiences as a "colored" girl growing up in apartheid-era South Africa radicalized her in ways that surely impacted the minds and personalities of her unconventional daughters. And her father, not just any man, but a Pakistani man, and a Pathan at that! The most conservative of tribes gave him his enviable whiteness and long, muscular legs (he was, remember, a tall man, whose military career further enhanced the muscled Pathani physique, suitable for men who live the hard life of mountain folk). Clearly, he was a *khar-dimagh*—a man with an uncommonly stubborn, don't-give-a-shit-about-what-anyone-thinks streak; a man who valued a woman with a brain in lieu of beauty, imagine! An unusual man by any standard, but one, I hear, given to bursts of uncontrollable rage, during one of which he fired a gun at a boy he thought was out to besmirch his eldest daughter Madina's honor, Madina, named after a city sacred to Muslims, Madina who was then all of nine-and-a-quarter years old. Soon thereafter he dropped dead of a heart attack, or perhaps an excess of bile. No one really knows.

Maddy's baby sister is Pakistan's answer to the ballooning beauty of Liz Taylor. I could tell you a thing or two about that Fareeha, oh yes, how, for instance, she was rumored to be a favorite of our beloved President Musharraf (or should I call him *Bush*arraf)—how her extraordinary tantrums caused the cinematically inclined brothers to spend the entire decade of the 1970s filming a movie in which she stars as a doe-eyed virgin who becomes the love object of a tribal dope smuggler with a heart of gold, an entire decade because she gave them all such a hard time—how she married first for love, then divorced, then married a plastic surgeon who lived oceans away while she spent her time filming the seamier side of life in Lahore. Suffice it to say, however, that I was as smitten by her arrogant beauty as I was by her older sister's flair for the dramatic. "I hate her," Fareeha says calmly. "Madina is a bloody bitch, a madwoman who thinks nothing of insulting her mother, brother, and sister on a daily basis. I don't know how you can possibly be her friend," this, with a glance that withers me with its scorn, " . . . mark my words, she will betray you the second you are of no use to her . . . tell her to get lost, fuck off," all of which I convey in as delicate a fashion as possible to Mad in the adjoining room where the ceiling fan is making a screeching sound I wish could stop.

"What did she say? *What did that hussy say?*" screams Madina, the decibel level of her voice drowning out the screeching fan. "I'm gonna gouge out her eyes, tear out her tongue, hack off her breasts, pull out every strand of hair in her head that lying, scheming *whore* . . ." Spluttering gobs of spit fly everywhere and I try and duck them unsuccessfully. "Go on, tell her, *tell her* what I'm saying, every word . . ." I run out before she shoves me out the two-paneled door. Breathless, wiping Mad's clammy spit off my cheek, I plead with Fareeha, "Your sister loves you; look, she's just a little upset because you didn't praise her directorial debut, you know how she values your opinion and thinks you are so lovely and really you are sisters, you shouldn't fight so much, think of your poor mother . . ." I sound trite and lame even to myself, an edge of desperation to my voice as I wonder at this pathetic role I find myself playing, me, who only ever wanted to star in my own show.

Fareeha cocks an icily raised eyebrow at me and permits herself a sardonic smile. "She's just jealous of me, you know. That's all. Don't you agree?"

Who can resist the dazzling row of pearls she flashes at the fortunate? Not me. I mutter, Judas-like, "Yes, yes, I do see," and then, to redeem my betrayal, "but please, can you just make peace, now that you and I understand what causes your sister to behave the way she does toward you. . . ." My voice trails off in a note of hope, and taking the slight nod of her regal head as a promising sign, I race out before she can accuse me of misinterpreting her signals. "Maddy, my dear," I fawn like the serf I am in this drama, "she says she's sorry and that she wants to make up with you."

Madina, ever gracious in her moments of victory, smiles with a sweetness that has never ceased to amaze me. "Why of course; she is my baby sister, I love her, what do you think . . . I know it's hard for her to have such a talented older sister, she has always felt threatened by me, poor thing, and she thinks Ammie loves me more and I know how that hurts her. It isn't true, but perception is everything. I know she is upset because my direction of *Blood Wedding* has won so many rave reviews, and she, poor thing, is just going nowhere in her acting career. How many times I've told her to come act for me, to stop wasting her time with those third-rate, shiftless, corrupt, money-grabbing bullshit artists, those P . . . assholes . . ." Her object of venom shifted, Mad opens the dividing door between her bedroom and Fareeha's, and with a lavish gesture of outstretched arms straight out of a Punjabi Lollywood movie, she embraces her sister.

I never have forgiven my parents for not letting me act in *Blood Wedding*. Mad's final year at Kinnaird College for Women, the spring of 1975, and she actually asks me to perform for her! Oh, the glory I could have had, and the fun I missed out on! And to have been part of an outlaw experiment, since Mad's production was not permitted to be performed on the main stage, for fear of the competition it might—and did—offer the long-standing resident director. In typical Maddy fashion, she refused to take no for an answer and proceeded to claim the outdoor stage where no plays had ever been performed, as her special space. Still, I got my own back years later. As a respectably married woman, with my reputation no longer my parents' responsibility, I returned to Lahore in the spring of 1987 to perform—finally!—in a role that seems to have been tailor-made for me. The play, in which I was now the madwoman, was written by a man who became Madina's third husband and in-house playwright for the company she founded in the mid-1980s, a time of unparalleled cultural and political repression under the military dictatorship of the late Zia-ul-Haq, to whom we owe thanks for the rise of Islamic extremism in Pakistan—an extremism that passed laws that targeted religious minorities and most visibly curtailed the rights of women of all classes.

But I get ahead of myself. It is 1978, our charming, putatively socialist prime minister is still in power, Zulfi the populist whose overconfidence will cost him his life, and I am freshly enrolled in the masters program for English literature at Government College, my first time ever in a co-ed institution. Government College, that venerable institution, beloved of Ravians—as all attendees are called, in deference to the once-roaring waters of the Ravi River that flows in the vicinity—and where we, playing hooky once or twice, tried to paddle canoes but got caught in the sandbars because the waters were so pitiably shallow. Madina, who took off to China to study Mandarin after she graduated two years ago from Kinnaird, has also joined the masters program, even though she is senior to most of us fresh baccalaureates.

It is the first day of classes, and already the air is thick with stories of Mad's scandalous behavior abroad. "Did you know she became . . . you know . . . , with a Chinaman, imagine, and she's had . . . , tobah, tobah," I overhear the whispered gossip wending its way from one end of the classroom to the other. "But listen, *yaar*," says Samina to Nuzhat in what could only be described as a stage whisper, loud enough for all the audience to hear, "she still got this nice *desi* man to marry her, despite the shame!"

"Haan, haan," Nuzhat chimes in loud and clear. "He's got a pretty good civil service job, *yaar*, and he's so sweeet-looking, like Hazrat Eisa." Apart from the fact that he is tall and thin and sports a straggly brown beard I have no idea why these girls think Sunny resembles Christ, but I suppose anyone married to Mad would need the patience of a saint if not a prophet. I'm looking forward to seeing Mad again, not having been in touch for these past two years. Will she have changed? I wonder a bit apprehensively.

I needn't have worried. She walks in wearing a white cotton saree with a jamun-colored border and scissor-toed slippers, her wavy hair tied in a severe knot at the base of her neck, her trademark unibrow glowering at us all, as she unceremoniously plonks herself down on the first-row bench, even though there are already three girls occupying it. "I can't walk all the way to the back because I am wearing a saree," she offers by way of explanation, and, sure enough, one of the girls vacates her seat just as the professor walks in. Poor Samina is asked to explain why she isn't already seated like everyone else. As she stammers a response, Mad smiles her violet sweetness while the boys in the back row look visibly uncomfortable. The big one with even bigger eyes simply stares, and when I glance his way I realize that it isn't Maddy he's staring at, but me.

We take up as though she'd never been gone. But something has changed. Maybe it's the eyes, I think; they seem, I don't know, just different somehow. Veiled in a way, shielding a secret, I begin to imagine, but what? The subject of her Chinaman never comes up; one wouldn't dare broach it in her presence. Oh no, some things you never bring up with She-who-must-be-obeyed, though your own private life is never off limits to her. "So, do you like him?" she looks at me slyly, "Blackbeard has clearly got the hots for you, just look at him stare at you all the time! Be careful he doesn't lock you in his chamber and chop your head off after he's made you suck his cock, wow, judging by his size that thing between his thighs has got to be humongous, hee hee hee!"

Her language and cackling have grown more vulgar; she's taken to using vernacular idiom that sounds horrifically obscene to my English-medium ears. "Fawzia's going to lulli put, lulli put," she chants and chortles like a sex-crazed adolescent boy from Bhatti Gate where all the lower-class people live, except, of course, she's punning on *Gulliver's Travels*, clever mixture of high and low, English education and Punjabi living that she is. Tarannum, the new best friend I've acquired at GC, laughs raucously, immensely enjoying Mad's vulgarity, while I, newly conscious of having turned into an elegant swan, refuse to be drawn in to the hilarity. "He can't even speak, just stares like an oaf, you can't seriously think I'd be interested in him, do you? And please stop talking all this sex stuff, I find it most distasteful. . . ." My voice is drowned out by a fresh wave of loud laughter that draws the attention of all the other boys and girls enjoying a tea break in the winter sun on the steps of the department verandah. Somewhat apart stands the object of our mirth, unabashedly staring me down, his body draped in a black khaddar shawl casting a giant shadow on the red-brick wall behind him. I toss my head in embarrassment, pride, disgust, I cannot tell which, and, turning my back on the merriment and the piercing stares, walk back up the steps into the coolness of the classroom.

Since she doesn't usually sport sunglasses, it's a little weird to see her come in, even in the already-90-degree heat of a punishing sunny day in May, uncharacteristically late to class at that, wearing Jackie-O sized goggles and what seems to have become her favorite type of dress. This time it's an off-white sari with a rich red border, dark enough to be almost purple, staining the white like a bloodstain left by cherries or jamuns, take your pick. "Whaaat is tha matter, sweet ladies and good gentlemen of Lahore, you seem vaary distracted this morning," declaims our Shakespeare professor Mr. Rehan, seeing us turn our gazes away from him. Shaking his index finger at Mad, he asks in a tone meant to be reprimanding, even sarcastic, but that comes out sounding oddly plaintive, "Perhaps Lady Madina of TV fame would care to explain her late arrival causing rude interruption please, yes, maybe you are thinking because you are big TV star now we will forgive your lateness, but, *beti*, you are like my daughter and I don't want you to miss any part of the important lecture," pleading now, "you are so bright, we must ensure your first-class position, so please, if you don't mind to try to be on time, yes? We are so honored to have you here . . ."

He blinks ingratiatingly behind those thick, black-rimmed lenses, and wouldn't you know it, Madina shoots back, "Mr. Rehan, sir, how dare you presume to question my lateness. I am late not because of my acting job on TV but because my husband beat me this morning. Have you no sensitivity, no shame, sir, in accusing a poor, battered woman of deliberately coming late to your class? Is this my fate"—turning to us now, she pulls the dark glasses off her face in a sweeping gesture— "battered at home, and now here at college? Is there to be no place of refuge for me, no respite from the cruelty of men?"

"Oh, lady, lady, dear Madam, my daughter," poor Rehan sahib, tripping over his mixed-up terms of address, exclaims abjectly, "I am sorry, I am sorry, oh dear oh dear, I know not what to say, this is a dark moment, we are with you . . . class dismissed." Bowing and scraping as though he were a minor character on a Shakespearian stage, Mr. Rehan, who hardly looks capable of swatting a fly, makes his exit, to leave the rest of us to gape and gawk at the blue-black bruises Madina shows off to us: first around her eyes, then the area exposed between the blouse and the petticoat of the saree. Who knows which other parts of her body she would have made us witness, the presence of the opposite sex clearly not daunting her, had Mr. Aftab not sailed in early to direct our attention to Greek Tragedy.

I cannot quite believe it. Neither can Tarannum. As we sit in the shade of the big neem tree after class, devouring hot spicy samosas and sipping ice-cold orange Mirindas, Tarranum reasons, "*Yaar*, how is this possible? That lily-livered Sunny, I can't imagine him, of all people, hitting this Amazon; I think it must be the other way around, she's got to be smacking him around. Maybe she's making this up so we can feel sorry for her instead!" Thrilled with her powers of deduction, Tarannum begins to giggle, then catches my expression and stops. "I'm sorry, *yaar*, I know she's your friend, but think about it, she could crush that skinny Sunny between her thighs in a minute, ha ha," she winks at me. "You know what I mean . . . okay, okay, I'll stop now. . . ." She trails off, sensing my discomfort.

It's true Mad and I seem to have drifted apart, the crudeness of her personality more apparent, or just more of an issue with me now than in preceding years. Still, I am a loyal soul, and "those were real bruises, Tarannum," I retort with real anger. Perhaps it's the freshness of those images, or because I suddenly recall the way in which another close friend has changed herself from the outside in to conform to her beloved's image of the right kind of woman, that I feel a tightening in my chest, like a skein of wool being gathered back in.

"Look, there is Mr. Big, devouring you with his eyes again." Rolling her own, Tarannum moans only half-jestingly. "How come no one ever looks at me like that?"

I turn, and ever so slightly, I give a nod in his direction.

HIM:
There you stand
on those steps
on that hot summer's day
Such a dream come true
Ghalib's saqi, my muse

With a toss of your head
and a swing of your hips
how you hiss, stomping off
oh my love
sweet young love

when you say in that way
what's the matter with you
has the cat got your tongue?

I wish then that the earth
would swallow me whole
chador, beard, passion
All

HER:
I'd rather *be* Ghalib
and/not his damned saqi
Writing those poems
yes inspiring those rhyme schemes

I don't want to give up
my power you see

so I'll be my own
slave, thank you, pretty please

but remember
dear departed
there always shall be
that question to consider
when our souls clash again

what shall we both do
having written our ghazals
always already
so hopeless, so silly
Imagining Forever
being Mad about Me.
              He never stood a chance.

After a year of pursuing my doctorate in America, having jilted
Khadim Bakri in a manner satisfying only to one who adores the feel
of crushed ice burning holes in her teeth, I heard through Tarannum
that he and Madina had tied the knot. It was the beginning of summer
session, and I was surprised, I think. In my new life as a graduate student in Massachusetts, I hadn't had much time to think about GC days
much, or anything else really except getting through my courses, which
were taught so differently and expected a whole new set of skills from
me. Well, that's not quite true. I had gone out on many dates—how
could I not, coming from a place where that sort of thing could only
be done on the down-low? I'd also organized an international fashion
show during my first semester in the fall, with the help of my under-
graduate roommate Debbie, in aid of Afghan refugees streaming into
Pakistan as the USSR invaded their country. That was when I'd first
met the man who became my husband, since we needed someone with

a car, even a beat-up one, to pick up and return clothes from Boston's fashionista stores.

I fell in love with him over winter break, waiting in line for Steve's ice cream during my first snowstorm. He picked me up on a Saturday evening, after I'd just finished the first draft of my master's thesis on Edith Wharton's novella *Ethan Frome*. We stood for an hour in the freezing cold of a Boston winter night, the windchill factor and swirling snowflakes pushing me ever closer to him to grab some body heat, until finally, he put his arm around me and we giggled all the way through the ice cream sundae we shared, hot despite the cold.

It was American-style love, yes; I sent him a giant valentine that spring and bought him a long coat to hang on his lanky frame. "You look like Omar Sharif," I said with stars in my eyes, while the pack of Paki boys he lived with shook with wicked glee. Okay, so I had bought it at Bowl and Board and who knows who had lived in it before it got to my Intended, but still, no reason to make fun of a poor girl just because she's a Paki too, "a *desi* trying to act *amriki*," I could just see the laughter in their eyes. He never did wear that coat, but he did marry me. After I proposed, of course—in the dawn following a night when we stayed up arguing whether Jorge Luis Borges' short story "The Garden of Forking Paths" was a challenge to Einstein's theory of relativity. Being a Ph.D. student in solid state physics at MIT, he had an edge over me there that I must have been an idiot to think I could beat. But try I did—and having exhausted his scientific logic with my mad energy and most unreasonable reason— well, dear reader, I got him to laugh at me, love me, and agree to marry me. We had a big wedding back home even though his father had no money. On our wedding day my mother broke her arm trying to fix a leaky toilet, his sister accused their brother of molesting her little girls, and my grandfather only half-jestingly warned him about a wife who strode out ahead of him. If this were a novel—which it's not—one might have said of our beginnings as a couple were rife with metaphor.

"Madina pursued me," proffers Bakri by way of voluntary explanation. We're lying in a bed in Bath, in a quaint inn in a quaint village, a destination to which our colonial education has led us most logically. I'm faintly bored by his need to explain, his search for redemption, which is not in my power to give. In any case, I need to worry about my own. But I listen. This is what I hear.

Bedroom scene in Madina's first husband's house; Fawzia and she quite grown up now

HUSBAND#1: Bloody bitch on wheels screaming virago cuntface screwingmachine take this thwackthwackthwack

MADINA: Behenchod, choothiasisterfucker I am Mad ina, Mad/ea don't mess with me

MY BITE IS WORSE THAN MY BARF

spitting venom in his face I'll scratch up that prettyboy face of yours jesus christ my ass HOW YOU HAVE FOOLED THEM
and don't forget my
sisterfriendsexysoulmate FAWZIA
she's good in a catfight you'd like that wouldn't you *cacklecacklechortle*

THWACK THWACK THWACK THWACK THWACK THWACK

in the Government College compound the next day 110 degrees Fahrenheit

CHORUS OF GOVERNMENT COLLEGE STUDENTS: the clock is ticking

time's a-passing
Mack the Knife is back in town
singing in the sweat
allah-hoo hooallahahoo
Mad-dy Maddy Quite Contrite-ly
why won't your marriage work
Maddymaddy Quite Cunt-rightly
you've made your bed of thorns

Now lay in it BITCH

Enter Fawzia followed by Bakri the Beard, a not-quite mullah devouring her with his BIGBIG eyes; a typical B(h)ollywood scene

BAKRI: there you stand on those steps
on a hot summer day
the Loo of Lahore makes my dream come true
Ghalib's saqi is my muse too

with a toss of your hair
and a swing of your hips
you hiss stomping off

FAWZIA: what's the matter with you has the cat got your tongue?

BAKRI: I wish the earth would
sWallow me (w)Hole
chadorbeardpassionall

FAWZIA: arreyyaar what is this
love/shove/ishq/vishq

get a-hold getagrip
this love-in-cholera isn't all

ALL: there is
strains of chura lyia hai dil ko jo tum nain, you who have stolen my
heart, from a popular Bollywood musical, play in the background

I'd rather be Ghalib
and not his damned Saqi
writing those poems
yes inspiring those rhymeschemes

I don't want to give up
my power you see
so I'll be my own slave
thank you *pretty please*

Fawzia stomps off tossing her head. Bakri watches and waits for the
duration of the play alternately weeping and jerking off, laughing and
jerking off, playing the sitar and jerking off, drinking and jerking off,
fucking Madina and jerking off. He becomes Madina's second hus-
band as Fawzia disappears to enter a different land(e)scape: London,
New York, Berlin cityscapes of the Other.

MADINA: eat my cuntlike you did
in the early dayswhydon'tyou
sonofabitchwhatsgotten in to you

BAKRI: you are a whore not a woman
eating the entrails of shellfish
you crunch to the marrow then spit out like a peasant

aren't you ashamed
of how FAT you've become eatingdrinking like there's no tomorrow

*Fawzia, I am COMing to Janat-ul-Amrika whyohwhy did you leave
me in this refuse heap of La(w)hori history with a madwoman*

Bakri turned Khadim shudders. I pull up the sheets to cover him, following the female tradition of the East, at least in this instance. Drama is
such good diversion. "I'm telling you, she's not a woman. She's a, a, I don't
know, something else, too terrible to name. Have you seen her eat lately?
If it can be called that. I'm telling you, when I saw her devour plate after
plate of food in Dacca, and then put the entire lobster whole in her mouth,
whiskers, eyes, everything"—I'm laughing now, in spite of myself—"no I'm
telling you, there is no exaggeration here." He suddenly turns quiet, those
big eyes clouding over, no beard to hide the unmistakable quivering of his
chin. "Come on, *yaar,*" I smile at him, "relax, shake off this Mad obsession,
you're with me, remember?" But there's no shaking her out of him.

I piece together the story in dribs and drabs. I realize I was the conduit
for an early exchange of love letters between Maddy and her third husband-to-be when I dropped off at his London apartment en route to New
York from Lahore what I thought was just a videotape. It was a record-
ing of the Lahore premiere of his first play performed by Mad's theatre
group on International Women's Day in 1987. "You are perfect as the
madwoman, and I very much like your vocal rendition of Bulleh Shah's
mystical verse; such a powerful voice you have." Even as I acknowledge
his praise for my work, my first—and last—dramatic role on a Lahori
stage, I realize as we watch the tape together that it's really Mad's performance as the husband-murdering adulteress that he's interested in.
Yes, she did direct herself well, but then, I think wryly, the role seemed

so fitting, somehow. We both look at each other at the moment she is wielding her axe on the TV screen, and he admits with a boyish grin so charming on an older man, "I did write that with her in mind."

Still, I think nothing of it, for matters more weighty than romantic love are on my mind, as they are for just about everyone that I know of within the Pakistani intelligentsia and particularly among those concerned with the fate of secular democracy and women's rights under Zia's increasingly alarming Islamist regime.

The play I had just finished performing in as member of Mad's new theater group was written by Salman while he was an exile in London, in danger of being arrested in Pakistan for what the military state considered his seditious activities. He was a student leader during Z. A. Bhutto's government, a People's Party union leader, a threat therefore to the illegitimate military dictatorship of Zia. From his office at Amnesty International, he penned this play about the lives of four female inmates of a Pakistani prison during Zia's rule. A horrific tale, of women beaten, raped, and tortured in their homes, on the streets and inside the jail cells. One woman wreaks vengeance against a system that gives her no rights by killing the eighty-year-old man who beats her daily after she is forced to marry him at the age of seventeen; another is raped and impregnated by prison guards after she is thrown in for the crime of dancing on a sufi saint's shrine, since dancing and singing by women is forbidden according to the Shari'a laws being rammed through the previously secular legal system of Pakistan by the Ruler of God's henchmen.

Indeed, several cases that had come to light in the months and years prior to the play being written and several that happened shortly after its first performance on the lawns of the Goethe Institute in Lahore illustrated, almost uncannily, the horrifying turn the country of my birth had taken vis-à-vis women's rights in the years since Zia-ul-Haq had taken power. Hamza Alavi, a Pakistani scholar tracking the legacy of Zia's regime, highlights some of the most egregious of these cases. He writes,

The most notorious case is that of Safia Bibi, an 18 year old virtu-ally blind girl, the daughter of a poor peasant, who was employed in the house of the local landlord as domestic help. She was raped by her employer's son and then by the landlord himself. As a result the girl became pregnant. Her illegitimate child is said to have died soon after birth. The girl's father filed a case with the police alleging rape. The Court acquitted the landlord and his son for lack of evidence as required under the Zina Ordinance, the evidence of the girl not being admissible and four *pious* Muslim witnesses to the repeated acts of rape not being available. But by virtue of her accusation the girl her-self, being unmarried, was found guilty of zina, her pregnancy being proof of it, and she was sentenced to three years in prison, public lash-ing (15 lashes) and Rs. 1000 fine. In passing this sentence, the Court said that it was being lenient in view of her age and disability! This case created an uproar and turned out to be an issue on which the Women's Action Forum began campaigning. In the light of public outrage, General Zia himself intervened and got the Federal Shariat Court to take over the case, *suo moto*. An exceptionally liberal judge quashed the outrageous conviction of the girl on the ground that if in the case of rape the man (or men) were acquitted due to lack of the required evidence, the woman too was to be given the benefit of doubt. But there was no question here of prosecuting the rapists and bringing them to justice.[1]

1. In a comprehensive essay on the ways in which the Islamization policies put into effect by General Zia-ul-Haq curtailed women's rights in the decade of the 1980s and have affected them negatively ever since, Hamza Alavi describes in detail the effects of the passing of the Hudood Ordinance of 1979. One can see that the play *Barri* was based on women whose plights echoed those of real women in the society at large. Maryam, the "madwoman" character I played, is thrown into jail because she is unattached to a man, i.e., has no male *saya* or protection against the forces of those who would imprison her. Once in, she faces the charge of *zina* or adultery, except that because she becomes pregnant while incarcerated, the jailers would have had a hard time explaining who she

A year after the play was first performed, a judicial panel of Islamic scholars heard arguments about Pakistani laws that accord the legal testimony of women half the weight of the testimony of men. Back in New

---

committed *zina* with. No wonder, then, that the baby she is carrying is forcibly aborted. The main protagonist is a character who faces another set of challenges—those of women who are forced into marriages, and then wishing to escape from them, find no legal avenue of escape.

Alavi describes one such case that has parallels to the main character: "A rather different type of case illustrates the way in which the law is used by male relatives or husbands to terrorise and control women. A young woman of 25, Shahida, got a divorce from her husband, Khushi Mohammad. The divorce deed was signed by the husband and was attested by a Magistrate. Under the law as it stands, however, the divorcing husband is then required to register the divorce papers with the local council. That he did not do. This was possibly a deliberate omission which was to give him a hold over his ex-wife. Shahida, after spending the prescribed period of ninety six days of waiting (*iddat*), as prescribed for a divorcee, with her parents, married Mohammed Sarwar. Khushi Mohammad, meanwhile decided that he wanted her back or, in any case, he would not allow her to marry again. So he took the matter to the law, charging her with *zina*. Although Shahida produced before the Court the attested copy of the divorce document which was signed by Khushi Mohammad and attested by a magistrate, the Court did not consider it to be admissible as it had not been registered with the local Council. The Court decided that the divorce was invalid and therefore that the second marriage illegal. As the two accused, Shahida Parveen and Mohammed Sarwar had 'confessed' to living together as husband and wife, the Court found them guilty, under the convoluted provisions of that extra-ordinary Ordinance, of raping each other! Accordingly they were both sentenced to stoning to death. Happily, due to campaigning by the women's movement that extreme sentence was eventually commuted—but not all victims of this extraordinary law have been so lucky" (Hamza Alavi, "Pakistani Women in a Changing Society," http://ourworld.compuserve.com/homepages/sangat/pakwomen.htm). In the play, the woman is not so lucky. The only way she can rebel is by murdering the husband who won't release her from a loveless and abusive marriage, and the man she falls in love with deserts her. She is incarcerated and subsequently executed for her "crime."

York, my blood boils when I read in the *New York Times* that a Muslim clergyman at the hearing asserted that women were emotional and irritable, with inferior faculties of reason and memory. He said courts were justified in discounting their testimony along with that of "the blind, handicapped, lunatics and children." It was precisely to counter such anti-women prejudices and laws being enacted against them as a consequence of such beliefs that Salman wrote the play that ended up bringing us all together.

I don't know it then, but this is the beginning of a beautiful relationship. "Here's looking at you, kids," Bogey might as well have said to buck Mad and me up in the coming decade. She directs plays on every aspect of the grave situation unfolding in Pakistan, I chronicle them in my scholarly essays and poems. Helping her build her troupe into a first-of-its-kind, leading theater company of Pakistan, a paradoxical presence on an extremist landscape, is her new husband, the Man from London.

"She turned him mad, you know," Tarannum turns to me conspiratorially as we sit cracking open peanuts on a lazy Friday afternoon at her gilded new house on the other side of the railway tracks from my parents' modest bungalow in Lahore. I am visiting again, on my annual December trip between semesters. "Friday is now the day off from work, no more weekends, it's the Islamic way," says T in her working-woman mode, rolling her eyes in that familiar way. "Anyway, as I was saying, . . . *ki hogya thuanoon,* Riaz baba, Pino," leaving the tale hanging in suspense, she excuses herself to chase down the good-for-nothing cook and gal Friday to get them to serve us lunch in her modern kitchen where no food is cooked by the servants. "Oh no," she explains, "they have their own kitchen, outside; this one is only for me and hubby and the kids to use when we feel like cooking."

"And how often is that?" I ask sarcastically. "Once a year?"

She nods, laughing in typical T style, a laugh so loud and raucous that even ten years of marriage to a *khar-dimagh* Pathan man hasn't succeeded in toning it down. "It's a good thing Hubby is out of town for the day on business and the boys are with their uncle and cousins, so we can be together, alone." She gives me a generous hug now, reminds me to call my mother and make sure my son is okay, so we can settle in to a nice, long, uninterrupted chat about our favorite characters.

"Oh no, *yaar*, this seems too much like a bad Bollywood movie. Come on," I protest, "you're asking me to believe that a big man like Khadim Bakri allowed himself to be bullied into madness, I mean real insanity by our beloved Madina?"

Shrugging off my incredulity, T continues undeterred. "I'm telling you, don't believe if you don't want—"

"Okay, but how do you know this?" I butt in.

"What do you think, these things can stay hidden?" she retorts, at which I wonder if she knows about Bath too; that could be sticky.

"All right, go on," I say hurriedly now, "I do have to be getting back soon."

"Well, during the last few months of their two years when she was studying drama at the university in Nottingham, he finally couldn't take it anymore. He says she was abusive beyond belief, even broke his sitar one night in a fit of rage." Tarannum is in top storytelling form now; I can see she is relishing the tale even as there's no doubt she feels immense compassion for the sorry figure Bakri cuts in it. "So one night, maybe the same when she broke his instrument, he leaves the house at some unearthly hour, stark naked." She pauses to observe the effect of this statement. I am satisfyingly aghast. She continues. "Apparently it was very chilly, even in May, and Maddy found him the next morning, after his disappearance caused her to run distractedly all over Nottingham looking for him." I have a hard time envisioning Mad in the role of worried wife, but okay, "well, she found him, stark naked," she repeats, "under a lamppost in front of the insane asylum." Since this happens to be in the area they lived, I don't think Madina had to look too far or hard, certainly not all over Nottingham. And why no one found him before Mad arrived on the scene remains a mystery; it appears he allowed himself to be led like a lamb by his wife into the institution for the mentally ill, where he stayed for a month. Upon his return to the world of the sane, he discovered he was a free man. His wife had filed for divorce.

Years later, I am at home after a particularly grueling day of teaching and almost don't answer the phone's insistent ring. It's him. I've heard about the divorce, of course I have, but it's been quite a while since our paths have crossed. "I thought I'd do a Ph.D. in musicology, and the government gave me a handsome stipend to come here to the University of London." Okay, I say, that's good. "Oh yes," he replies. "Besides, I couldn't let you be the only doctor in our group," I can almost hear him smiling. His voice, with the old hesitance gone, irritates me for some reason. "Have you read *Love and Death in the Time of Cholera*?" he asks and when I say no, though I have, his disappointment is palpable over the phone lines. "It's our story, you know," and as soon as he says that, right on cue, I am enraged and, telling him I have to go practice my singing, abruptly hang up.

"First, he has to take up the sitar to compete against my singing," I find myself thinking narcissistically, while I try playing the attentive wife and mother over dinner a little later. "Then, he has to marry the woman who was *my* friend, not his," okay, that sounds weird even to me, "now he has to get a Ph.D. just because I have one!" What I'm really steaming at, I admit to myself much later, is the enormity of his arrogance at still desiring me.

⁂

Your fingers are so perfect I like their tapered form, long, elegant like your neck, and the daintiest of feet toes painted red matching your lips and the cleft in your chin ever so slight your nose ohmylady with the recently acquired diamond glinting in the sun your eyes kohl-rimmed oases a man can rest in trekking across a thirsty desert by god when I first saw your picture in the papers announcing your second position in the BA exams in the Punjab province I knew you were what our poets had been writing about all these centuries the perfection I had been searching for when I read you were enrolling in the English lit masters program at GC I knew that's where my destiny lay . . .

The clichés finally catch up with me, at the end of a long season of drought. But droughts end, and incessant rain becomes oppressive. I am glad I am escaping the summer heat of Lahore despite the delight of the monsoons, and going home after completing my research on street theater in contemporary Pakistan. It's been great fun hanging out with Maddy and the players, and everyone else besides. Now it's time to return to my life in the States, via a stop in London to visit my brother for a few days and a side trip to Bath for a day to reminisce about Chaucer. I smile to myself in the plane, recalling how *The Canterbury Tales* were taught us by gap-toothed Professor Ramzi, who always took care to wrap his one remaining strand of hair all the way around his cone-shaped skull, a piece of hair that caused greater merriment among us when it came undone and flopped around during his animated lectures than did the X-rated antics of the Wife of Bath.

I'm so enraged that he's followed me home, I drive him around very fast in my little red Jeep the color of fresh-spilled blood, round and round the twisting, hairpin bends in the mountains where I live, blaring music he begs me to switch off. One day, I find myself on a city street with my colleague Paul with whom I've just been to see *The*

Cook, the Wife, the Lover, and the Thief. I've asked Bakri to meet me at the corner of the street across from the theater. There, en plein air, surrounded by strangers, having introduced him and Paul to each other, I say good-bye. Paul and I walk off, excitedly discussing the film, and if Bakri tries to wave, we don't see him. A month later, when I am away at a conference in Canada, I am told by my husband that he's called. I do not call him back.

Not too long afterwards, I come home from the university to a message on my machine. It's Tarannum's hubby, of all the people, not T, not Mad, but Tarannum's husband, calling to say he's sorry to tell me that our mutual friend Bakri, who only ever wanted to be a Khadim, is dead. He had just turned forty.

rage
continues
to grow

a man y
splendored—
lush
dark

it's thick foliage
a veritable rainforest
with
plummage rich

brightly colored birds
fantastic
deep hues greenbluered
blending then
se pa ra ting

the foliage provides cover
red screams
the birdsong

you see me
you don't

a forest
is difficult to
penetrate
the rainforest
so verdant
wet
ecologically speaking

He never did stand a chance. Madina stands, though, winner of the Pride of Performance, Pakistan's highest artistic award. Ironic that she should have been awarded this during a military dictatorship, given her principled stand against a prior undemocratic regime. I stand too, my research finally a published book on the importance of Mad's brand of theater on women's rights in contemporary Pakistan.

Seminar on Women and Development, Lahore

In the grand auditorium
next to Shirkat Gah
off Ferozepur Road near
Kalma Chowk in the
city of my birth, Lahore

I tear my hair out
whirling whirling

to the
songs of the sufis
banned
by military dictators with
Religion on their minds

Dictators, fundamentalists, guardians
of female honor
snatched my dancing girl
from her saint's shrine
beat her
cursed her
raped her
threw her in prison for her sinfulness

that became a bloated belly
what effrontery in an Islamic state
where only mullahs and military mustachioes
may drink and dance and do god's will
at private parties
the public mustn't find out about

And so;
twenty years later
here I am
at a seminar on
Women and Development
in the city of my birth
playing
the same old whore I did back then

La-hore hasn't changed much
I see

Mad/medea

the same familiar faces in the
audience of the auditorium
older
grayer
still clamoring for Human Rights
for themselves
for their daughters
for the poor
for the minorities

Pakistan is still in debt
to the IMF and the World Bank
another military dictator in thrall
to the mullahs
has replaced the one
from twenty years ago
both blessed
by the Greatest Secular Democracy
in the world

So you see
we still need these seminars
and street theater
on Women and Development
on my trips back home
to the developing world
I can count
on reprising
the mad dervish role of my youth

a comforting thought
for an aging actress.

Epilogue

It is a very hot evening in Lahore. It must have been June 7 or 8—because I do recall it was recorded as the hottest day in June that year—120° Fahrenheit at midday when I thought I would pass out after two hours without a fan because of the usual load-shedding. It wasn't too bad looking back—now, in 2008, Pakistan has even less energy resources to draw on, and while the super rich siphon off those meager resources via power generators that provide them with air-conditioned interiors around the clock—the majority of Pakistanis suffer without even a measly fan to get the hot stale air moving around them for as long as ten hours a day. Climate change has ensured that the long hot summers of places like Lahore have steadily gotten hotter—and longer.

Last year, I arrived in Lahore on June 8, just in time to meet another day just as hot as that one almost thirty years ago. Apparently, Lahore had not seen such high temperatures in a few years despite a slow incline upwards in the intervening decades—and at night, when Lahorites typically experience a little relief in temperatures, this June of 2007 wanted to bestow no such minor kindnesses. Having not returned to Lahore in the month of June since that long-ago one of 1979, the feeling of being trapped in a huge clay oven, like the tandoori roti I love to eat, was overpowering in the paradox of its awfulness softened in the afterglow of nostalgia.

⌘

I am being hustled—looking back, that is the most appropriate word to describe it, I think. Hussled by Haji, and her sister, so smoothly I don't even know it. It is my last night in Lahore before leaving for the southern city of Accra in Ghana with my younger brother. He and I, being at university and high school, had to finish out our school year before going off to the Dark Continent to join our parents. My dad is in his third year of posting there, as the "expert demographer" on loan from the government of Pakistan to the government of Ghana via the United Nations. What that means exactly I am not sure—but it has to do with someone from one "third world" nation (these are the days before we used the more politically correct appellation of "developing nations" to describe erstwhile colonies of Empire)—teaching his counterparts in other even less-developed countries, some of the skills seen as necessary to "development," collecting and collating data on population, education, health, and so on. Mum—who applied and got leave from the women's college where she teaches English literature—and my other brother who has Down syndrome, left to join Dad some months ago, and now it's Farhan's and my turn.

We will be gone for the duration of the official summer months—the rest of June, July, and August, and I am bummed out that none of the "gang" I have become close friends with through Haji—my boys as I like to think of them, being possibly more besotted with myself than they are—have thought to come and say goodbye to me or throw me a party or take me out for dinner . . . I mean *nothing!* Like I don't even exist, I whine to Haji, trying to pass self-importance off as legitimate hurt. Her patiently bemused look—come to think of it, my twenty-two-year-old daughter now looks at me the same way when I go on about some slight real or perceived—sets me on edge, and because I know I am being silly, I dig in my heels when she and Hayley insist that I get in their car and go say good-bye to dear old khala, their aunt, my aunt, everyone's cool khala who loves to sing at the drop of a hat in her deep throaty voice surprisingly strong despite its quivering quality.

I am not dressed, I moan, and I have *taile*—coconut oil—in my hair . . . oh, just put on some lipstick, the sisters say, rolling their eyes in almost identical fashion . . . but look at what I'm wearing I pull down the corners of my face . . . I secretly do like my African kitenga, like a maxi-dress, a riotous profusion of redblackgreenyellow surrounding the white V-shaped patch down the middle of the front and back, brown skinny arms sticking out from the space left unstitched on the sides. They are losing patience with me, I mean really, I can tell . . . ohplease-fawz, they say, one then the other. . . . who do you need to impress, Hayley asks laughing . . . It's almost 9 p.m., let's hurry up you know it's getting beyond Khala's bedtime . . . I mean, it's only Khala *yaar*, yawns Haji in her inimitable drawl . . . c'mie'onn'ie Madame Sin, upsy daisy . . . and we are in the car, the driver having waited patiently outside in the clammy evening still registering a stifling temperature of 95° Fahrenheit, with not even a whisper of wind to breathe some relief onto perpetually per-spiring bodies. . . .

∞

The heat has not broken at all through my two-week stay in Lahore. With no hint of even a dust storm in the offing that could spell a few degrees' lowering of temperatures, I climb aboard one of the air-conditioned

Korean-owned and operated buses that have become such a popular because reliable and inexpensive mode of transport between Lahore and Rawalpindi. I am excited, despite the enervating heat. I have—thanks to my friend the journalist with whom I experienced that unforgettable night of Ashura almost a decade ago—secured an interview with Ghazi Abdul Rashid, rector of the notorious Red Mosque, Lal Masjid, that has been the flashpoint of fundamentalist extremism at supposed logger-heads with the military establishment ruling Pakistan, and of course, the epitome of western fears about Islamist terrorism. He is the younger brother of Maulana Abdul Aziz, the overall head of the Red Mosque and its two madrassas—one seminary for men, the other, adjoining the Red Mosque, for women. I am to meet Aziz's wife (I don't yet know she is his wife) after interviewing Ghazi sahib.

She is the principal of the Jamia Hafsa—the female seminary—which shot into international prominence when pictures of its female seminarians were released on the Internet, wearing what came to be referred to as black ninja outfits—head-to-toe coverings, slits for eyes to peer through—and wielding tall bamboo sticks as they raided local video and music stores to destroy what they deemed as "porno" materials, so out of place in a Muslim country. There had been one incident not so long ago where the girls had dragged some poor older woman, a resident of Islamabad, out of her house and kept her prisoner inside their seminary for a while—trying to get her to recant her evil ways—accusing her of being a madame of a brothel. And just days before my arrival to interview the male head of the seminary and his female counterpart—Umm Hassan as she was popularly known—as well as some of the female students at Jamia Hafsa, there had been an international incident resolved just the night before my interview in which the female inmates had again gone off on one of their vigilante missions. They had captured some Chinese nationals who they claimed were running a brothel in the guise of a massage par-lor, then released them after a few days when the Chinese government intervened and the Pakistani generalissimo decided it was time to flex his muscles and get the release negotiated before he looked too weak or too much in thrall to the militants. . . .

Between the colonial remnants I grew up with as a convent schoolgirl back in the 1960s and '70s and this moment—this present-day obsession with religious militancy and the military elite, which had spawned the Islamist movement since the days of Zia-ul-Haq, and which Musharraf since 9/11 had been encouraging even as he spouted his rhetoric of Enlightened Moderation—this moment was fraught with personal sadness and other mixed-up emotions and realities that mocked me through the looking-glass of Pakistani politics, even as I realized I had been trying to come to terms with all that history as I entered the here and now of the woman I had become. Ah yes, dear reader, the irony of She-who-was-not-I, the Paki princess who had become a left-leaning American professor, the girl who had grown to know her strengths as a result of her friendships with her Pakistani girlfriends, and who now was a feminist because of those experiences, which had left most of them behind—and yet, and yet, who skulked, and hid, and flirted with the self-othering of swooning Victorian romancing girlishness even toward the end of her fourth decade, who felt her Muslimness as deeply as only one who has been raised in the faith and yet who hated the nonsense of religion with all her heart, and could see the dangerousness of the illusions it encouraged, including this awful case being presented to the Lahore High Court regarding a young couple whose marriage their parents wished to nullify on the grounds that the husband was actually a transgendered individual and hence their marriage was un-Islamic. . . . She, who took her activism as critic of injustice seriously here, and there, yet wanted to have her proverbial bread and eat it too—ah yes, such ironies did not escape me.

I settled into the four-hour bus ride through the outskirts of Lahore, onto the Grand Trunk Road, past colonial monuments and contemporary buildings, roadside mosques, vendor stalls selling fruits and vegetables and prayer mats, and doctors' clinics to remind me of my mother's battle with cancer unfolding on this strange trip, which also reminded me of my own brush with breast cancer a few years ago, and all the sightssmellssounds of the town and then the countryside whizzing past as the bus smoothed into its ride, recalling me back to that summer of '79 through the mystically painful love affair I was having with it in this moment . . .

GT Road Lahore
Kipling would not recognize it
Corollas
Kalma Chowk
Rickshaw men

On cement heaps
A billboard
Proclaims Kipling
Centre
Cadet College and the Female
Announcer begins
In the Name
Of Allah, the All Merciful
All-Knowing
"Dr. Watson, Chemist,"
How presumptuous I think
Old Chap
The post sitting cheek by
Jowl with the Neo
And we are an Islamic Republic,
Officially

"We have started our Journey
For
Rawalpindi" she says and

I see an International
Super Store on My
Left
Behind the coming
Meeting with the Militants
Some fruit
seller's stand
Trading the Quranic signboard
For customers willing to buy
Produce polluted
By the canal
Machine
Made
Carpets
Hang in front
Of the Black and White Minaret
Of some red
mosque
testament to the survival of
Afghans displaced
Global College of Commerce
We pass Globalization en route
To the Capital
Of Mullahs
As cars are lifted
By forklifts
For not parking
Where they
Are supposed to which is
Nowhere

Chughtai's Lahore Lab
On my left

Where Mum had her
cancer diagnosed
And I came to see her
And meet the traveler
Who needs to tell
Me of horses and Sufis
Next
To the Heart
And Body
Scan Clinic
Screaming at me

The color of blood
I see scattered
On these roads
As tires
Burn in riots
Against Rushdie
And electric
failures repeat
those of the
State meant to look
after its
Own

The mud
huts now
fortified by brick
in places look
so quaint
Still
in the middle of green
fields and buffaloes

splashing in
troughs
the pastoral
redeemed
lives on to
placate us

But I and you
You and I
Old Kipling and Rushdie
Repeat the neo
In the post
A game designed
To obliterate
the present unlivable
unliving
travelers on a journey to
no man's land

where s/he couples no
longer need a
name
and the red
mosque has no
color

and you
and I

I
And
You
Are glad

Epilogue

To be
The places
And colors
In between

Why is he blowing the horn? I ask Haji and Hayley, puzzled about the need for creating such ruckus after we have entered the driveway to Khala's house on that still summer night. Hayley cackles, "Maybe he wants to warn the potholes to get out of his way." I am not amused. I haven't even begun packing for my three months in Africa (unbeknownst to me, I will return to Lahore only briefly, then leave for good for the US of A)—the flight is less than twelve hours away, I am tired and hot and feeling decidedly unattractive, and really, did I have to be dragged into visiting Khala at the last minute? Trying to muster some grace, I put on a smile as I enter the living room at the right end of a longish corridor. The lights, as usual, are dim—Khala does not favor strong lights. There she is, dear old Khala, sitting on the single-seat sofa-chair whose faded upholstery has seen better days, facing the entrance to the room, the dining table behind her laid for four. I must say, I am a little disappointed. I had, you see, hoped against hope that perhaps, perchance, maybe the guys, our Fine Arts College buddies, my friends as much as they are Haji's—Riz the Whiz and Character and Machoo and Jeeroo—those guys, would be there, hiding in the shadows, jumping out to hug me with their "Surprise!" greeting . . . ooh, yes, I would so have liked that . . . and their nonchalant behavior all explained and redeemed then. But no, alas, it wasn't to be so. That is the way fancies go. I should get used to life's disappointments, I tell myself gravely. This is just a preparation for what all of us will have to face . . . disappointment in friends, then lovers, then spouses, then children . . . ok, ok . . . this train of thought sounded fatuous even to me, so with a genuine delight at seeing Khala so happy to see me, I throw my arms around her and plop down on the sofa next to her.

Haji goes off to get me a Coke . . . Bilal the cook is busy putting finishing touches to what Khala warns me will be a very simple meal; she, after all, can only digest boiled food at this late hour, although, she tells me sweetly, "I have asked Bilal to make you your favorite chicken cutlets." Just as we are settling in for a cozy chat, Hayley jumps up, exclaiming, "I think we should move outside to the back lawn . . . it's too damned hot in here, Khala. . . ." I am loathe to move, but seeing that Khala is in agreement and Haji is nodding too, I suppress a sigh and we all get up and walk toward the back door. That's when I see that the chicks—the straw screens covering the French windows of the living/dining room that open into the lawn, are still down.

"Why are the chicks still . . ." I begin in puzzlement when Haji thrusts me through the door she has just unlatched, and there, as I stumble and almost fall because of Haji's push, my questions about the chicks and the tooting horn are answered by a volley of whoops and hollers shouting, "Surprise!!!" There is confetti and colored rice being thrown at me and beautiful Chinese lanterns glittering like fireflies all over the lawn trees and bushes and maypoles—maypoles?!—strung with more paper lamps in all the colors I love—reds, oranges, mustard yellows, pinks, purples, and parrot greens. And the green-gray eyes of Sherry . . . strange they should be there, too, among the pairs of all those other dear eyes . . . she was not someone I considered a friend, or not a close one anyway . . . but she was one of the FAC in-group, and, I find out later, in a hot and heavy romance with my guitar-strumming Romeo . . . and also on her way to becoming a major star of television dramas beloved by Urdu-speaking Pakistani audiences.

She, and Haji, Hayley, another girl named Farhat in their group, myself—we were the women coming of age then, heralding a new progressive era for the women of Pakistan. And those boys we were friends with, had crushes on, beginning love affairs with—some to last a life-time, others to end in marriage—sometimes . . . well, at least on that sultry, sexy, evening steeped in the innocence and hope of our youth, I was happy, the center of attention, adoring friends around me, and me adoring them madly, they and I, I and they, connected through our connection to the land we had grown up in . . . a country barely a decade older than us, a nation that was going to grow in the direction of our dreams . . . I laughed and danced all night, despite the ickiness of oil in my hair. Yes, we were friends, and we were all going somewhere differ-ent, but somewhere exciting and full of promise. I could feel it coming in the hot night air.

⚬⚬⚬

June 27, 2007, a week before the Army Rangers move in to attack the Red Mosque and Jamia Hafsa inhabitants, I find myself inside their premises trying to make sense of how we got from the Pakistan I had inhabited that summer of 1979 to this Pakistan, so close to the precipice you could smell the danger of the edge about to explode in all of our faces in the furnace of the summer of 2007. Had I traveled across continents and time zones to get to the nowhere of this moment and this space that was so alien I craved the somewhere of an almost-forgotten intimacy, now forbidden fruit in the declining years of what-ifs? Maybe I and others of my ilk had neglected to see that Pakistan was not us, having made the fatal mistake privileged youth and attendant arrogance always does in placing itself center-stage.

So then . . . out of one portal and in through another . . . this one emblematic of the Pakistan made of corrugated rusting steel, with Quranic inscriptions in praise of the Holy Prophet and his companions adorning them. Inside, a large central space. "That is our reception area," explained one of the women I had followed, as she took off her burqa. There were two rooms leading off this space, and beyond, I could see a central courtyard, with corridors and what looked like rooms off the courtyard around it. Later, when I was taken on a tour of the seminary, I saw that the central courtyard had several doorways leading off from it and into the classrooms and living spaces of the boarders. Each of these doorways had inscriptions like *Baab-e-Syeda* and *Baab-e-Fatima* in multicolored calligraphy adorning them, indicating the sacredness of the space, each "door" a portal into the inner sanctum of female piety signed by the name of a female relative of the Prophet or his caliphs. Girls, women, mostly in their twenties and some younger walked about like normal students at a school going about their daily business. The atmosphere was hushed, and there were clutches of girls dressed in reds, pinks, and blues hanging about the courtyard or walking from one spot to another. Several looked up at this new presence entering the premises and simply stared. I was ushered into the room adjoining the reception area to my left.

There, in a modest-sized room, I am introduced to eight or nine women, half of them students, the others their teachers, who claim to be from all over Pakistan, including one from Azad Kashmir, a couple from NWFP, but the majority from around Rawalpindi and other areas of the Punjab. I am invited to sit on the one sofa in the room, and a soft drink is ordered for me—an orange Fanta. No one else gets one, nor asks—the two Pakistans we represent remain separated by a soft drink. Some slices of pound cake and cookies are also placed in front of me and then one student in particular, sporting a white hijab and thick reading glasses, zeroes in on me and begins talking nonstop.

It is, I must confess, a mesmerizing tactic. She discourses about many things, particularly economics, and before I know it, we are thick into Adam Smith's *The Wealth of Nations*. Amina Adeem, I think the student is called, very solemnly declared that it was Adam Smith—and other western economists and thinkers like him—who, because they were afraid of Muslims' combined collective strength, decided that the best way to avoid an Islamic revival was to promote an economic model that would ensnare the Muslim Ummah in money worship! The decadent lifestyle that invariably accompanies the worship of such an idol has transformed what should have been Dar-ul-Islam—the Land of Islam—into Dar-ul-Kufr, or the Land of Unbelievers.

"Look," she continues breathlessly, enthralled by the speed of her words tripping off her tongue, seeking to convert the infidel she sees in me, "at these rich disgusting men of our society today." I nod obligingly. "They are not happy, these rich men, despite many wives, mistresses, cars, guards . . ." This is news to me, but I try not to spoil her moment. She continues, now joined by a chorus of other voices, "Look at Abdul Rehman bin Arif," or, pipes another, Abu Obeida, and Abu Bin Jaraa, throws in another, not to be outdone.

"The point is," Amina hissed, her eyes glinting through her frames, "these Islamic leaders lived like ordinary folks. Their homes were never looted, they did not live in fear of dacoits. But here, today, here it is the rule of dacoits, and who suffers?" The other girls joined in unison, "It is ordinary folks like us who are suffering. . . . Who can afford mutton at 350 rupees a kilo?"

There is a sudden hush as a fair-complexioned woman, slightly stout but good-looking, wearing a gray-blue shalwar kameez and holding a young boy in her arms, enters the room and approaches our little menagerie. *"Asalam-o-alekum,"* she nods at the greeting of the students and the few teachers in their midst, and extends a hand to me. "Welcome, you must be the professor Ghazi Sahib sent our way." She sits down on the sofa next to me, and I inform her I had been having an informative chat with her students, but they wouldn't let me record them without her permission. "Oh no, I am afraid that is not allowed," she says firmly, and then, to my query if I might photograph them, she replies again in the negative, decisively.

"Not even with their burqas on?" I plead.

"No. Why objectify us like that? That would serve only a sensational purpose . . . and surely that is not why you are here?" She throws me a knowing glance, and I hasten to agree. This was not a woman you wanted to be on the wrong side of! She informs me she is a Punjabi—not a Pathan as one might assume, given her tall, fair carriage. She claims to have been in the school since 1992, the date that it came into existence, with herself as founder and principal to this day . . . that would make her tenure there almost fifteen years. But she is a young woman even now, maybe in her mid-thirties . . . with a small son in tow, whom she promptly hands over to one of the teachers and then devotes her attention to me and to the conversation I had been having with her prize students. Catching on quickly, she asks me, "What do you think a kilo of ghee costs? Rent for a family of four in a city? What does an ordinary mazdoor make on average in a day? Huh, memsahib?" She has sized me up fast. "Do you know that on one side of our madrassa are homes of the rich and the famous, and on the other side are whole colonies of jhugees? People living in tents, katchi abadis . . . and even in the rich houses, the poor servants are given the filthiest of quarters. . . ."

I try to counter her claims of dire straits of servants by pointing out that drivers, at least, made pretty good salaries . . . six thousand rupees a month. . . . My voice trails off as a blaze of laughter erupts.

"And do you know what it costs just to pay electric and water bills, provide school fees for your kids and some milk as nourishment? Oh Bibi ji . . ." and they pin me with bemused looks. "Just these few necessities add up to at least 4,000 rupees a month for a family of four, and that doesn't include rent or food or transportation or clothing. And how many of our average poor folks can even get jobs as drivers to big homes in the cities?"

Umm Hassan concludes, "We need economists schooled in the university of the Prophet. What need do we have of Ph.D.s from abroad when our own folks cannot find decent jobs?" As if to drive her insult home, she points out, "300 people commit suicide on average every month. Because," she explained, fixing her stare on me, "they have no jobs." Hmm . . . I thought back to my earlier conversation with Ghazi sahib. The figure he cited was 3,000 suicides annually. Clearly, the number 3 seemed important in their calculations. It is virtually impossible to get accurate figures about suicide since such data is not, and never has been, systematically collected by any Pakistani agency, government or otherwise. But clearly, she has a valid point; "the elite classes of this country think of the rural masses and the underclass simply as cockroaches, as chipkalis . . ." Her point was this: Lady, this conflict is about class. No wonder when I ask her why she has named herself "Umm Hassan," and why so many others used the same Arabic appellation, she shoots back ferociously, "Arrey, arrey arrey. . . . We love Arabs . . . we love our Prophet who was Arab, and so we take our names from them, just like," and her voice turns sarcastic as she looks me up and down, "just like some folks love Imran Khan and Lady Diana . . . so why criticize us?" Her "girls" laugh delightedly at a comment they had obviously heard before, separating "them" from the rest of "us" westernized, debauched elites.

And yet, paradoxically, Umm Hassan seems a stauncher women's libber, free of the yoke of husband and family, than any "westernized" Pakistani woman I'd ever met—including myself. "I would care not a whit if my husband left me tomorrow—he and all my other relatives don't want me in here, away from 'womanly' duties; they say they are so worried about me being in here. My sisters tell me they can't sleep at night worrying for my safety, thinking we'll be attacked by the police or army any day." Looking back, her remarks proved to be prescient. She smiled sardonically, "I tell them I'm not worried. I have no trouble sleeping. Because I know I'm on the right side. I fight for the victory of truth and justice. So I sleep like a baby."

I later find out that she is the wife of the head cleric of the Red Mosque and Jamia Hafsa, Maulana Abdul Aziz, the militant whom the military establishment sees as its chief nemesis, never mind that its own secret intelligence service—the ISI—is reputed to have helped the maulana and his outfit of Chicks with Sticks as well as their male counterparts build up their ammunition dump. During the debacle that ensued between the military and the militants following my departure for the USA after my interviews, Maulana Abdul Aziz was caught trying to escape the mosque by hiding under the cover of a burqa. Umm Hassan was eventually captured, but she stayed inside the Jamia Hafsa with her students and teachers till the bitter end, when they were forced to surrender after two or three hundred of their inmates had been killed by the Army (Pakistani government figures cite 102 inmates killed). She now lives in a house in a lane near the site of the Red Mosque and Jamia Hafsa—both razed to the ground in the summer of 2007—and spends much of her time attending the trial of her husband, who remains behind bars.[1] Her older son, a lad in his twenties, was killed in the operation. I interviewed her again in January 2008, shortly after the assassination of Benazir Bhutto. I am amazed at her calm and at her defense of her husband, whom she claims did nothing wrong and was wearing the burqa only because he had been asked to don it by military authorities when they requested him to come outside to begin negotiations with them. And then, "those bastards nailed him." She spat onto the ground in front of the house I visited her in. "I told him it was a ruse . . . that he shouldn't go out. He didn't listen to me."

And so, dear reader, it goes. I find myself wondering about the relationship between this radical Islamist woman and her husband, the maulana,

1. Maulana Abdul Aziz was released by the Pakistani Supreme Court on April 16, 2009, while still awaiting trail for murder, incitement, and kidnapping. While throngs of supporters greeted him, many civil society groups voiced their opposition to his release.

the leader. Contrary to media projections and common understanding, she is the one who seems to be more "in control" of situations than he. A woman so sure of her faith she does not observe marital niceties and obligations if to do so would take her away from her perceived mission—however insane to the rest of us—in the name of that faith. And I find myself thinking back to the accommodations to philandering husbands my saner, more secular-minded friends have had to make, all of them from a much more highly educated and socioeconomically privileged backgrounds than Umm Hassan. Even Sherry the TV star gave up her career to make her far-less-successful husband feel more "manly." And like Saira's H-bhai and Haji's Sufi—Sherry's itinerant, mystic-minded lover rewarded her sacrifice of self to gain his own . . . via the embraces of mistresses and their obliging servant girls.

Even Benazir is known to have put up with a reputed womanizer of a husband—he was referred to as the playboy of Karachi before they wedded—and later he embroiled her two short-lived governments in scandals of corruption, having earned the street sobriquet of "Mr. Ten Percent" for all the bribes he allegedly received from companies and individuals doing business in Pakistan. He may even—it is alleged— have physically abused her. And now, after her tragic death, it is he, the husband, who has taken over her political legacy with seeming ease. I find myself nodding with a sense of déjà vu when I read the following quote from the Pakistani columnist Nosheen Saeed:

With the NRO [the National Reconciliation Ordinance passed by Musharraf's government on October 4, 2007, allowing all former politicians to return to Pakistan with pending cases of corruption and so forth against them being dropped], Zardari has gained sole control of Benazir's assets and property; by becoming the PPP's co-chairperson he has taken over the reins of her party; by changing his name to Asif Bhutto Zardari he has hijacked Bhutto's political legacy and by becoming the leader of the largest party of Pakistan he is dreaming of occupying the Prime Minister and President houses in Islamabad. Is there anyone in the world who has benefited more from Benazir's death than Mr. Zardari?

So, I now find myself asking—could those Chicks with Sticks—as the sophisticated elite of Pakistan laughingly referred to them—have got some of their anger right?

So, I now find myself wondering, what will become of us—the children of my youth? My girlfriends—*piyari sahelian*—and the boys we loved, who grew up to be the men we love to hate? Do we really hate them? Or does love look like hate sometimes? Are we doomed to inhabiting this binary universe or can we challenge the system that turns us into the roles we wear like selves? And what about those other girls—those who were never *sahelian*—who lurk under covers I find threatening to my liberalism? How does one sort through the guilt that cohabitates with anger—how do we recognize our shadow selves, and make peace with our most intimate secret sharers?

I do not have the answers to these questions any more now than I did then, when I first began my journey into the world of questions without answers that lay outside myself and my tight circle of childhood girlfriends, waiting, like the bogeyman of nightmares, to snatch us and throw us into the vortex of life's complexities. Sometimes I wonder who it is of us all who succumbed to the dizzying pull of that spiral into the abyss of a self that is permanently dis-eased in the otherness of outsiderdom. Haji ended the tussle with a finality that has left open wounds that time, contrary to popular wisdom, has been unable to close. But she—like the other *sahelis*—never had to contend with the ever-multiplying fissures of a selfhood fractured into so many roles, performances of identity I am doomed to rehearse and repeat ad nauseum as I shuttle back and forth, back and forth between here and there, America and

Pakistan, my life as an academic, a scholar, a party girl, a mother, a daughter, a wife, a friend, a lover, an actorsingerpoetactivistmemoirist. Who am I? Why am I here? Where am I going? So many questions, so little time left, in a life that has become more and more that rusty steel seesaw I continue to ride like the little girl I once was in the company of my beloved *sahelian*.